KATHE S. DARBY, M.A.

Never Be Nervous Again

Never Be Nervous Again

The World-Renowned Speech Expert Reveals Her Time-Tested Method for Foolproof Control of Nervousness in Communicating Situations

by Dorothy Sarnoff

with Gaylen Moore

CROWN PUBLISHERS, INC. NEW YORK

To Milton

Published by Crown Publishers, Inc., 225 Park Avenue South, New York, New York 10003 and represented in Canada by the Canadian MANDA *Group.*

CROWN is a trademark of Crown Publishers, Inc. Manufactured in the United States of America Library of Congress Cataloging-in-Publication Data
Sarnoff, Dorothy.
   The World-Renowned Speech Expert Reveals Her Time-Tested Method for Foolproof Control of Nervousness in Communicating Situations
      1. Public speaking.   I. Moore, Gaylen.
II. Title.
PN4121.S2768   1987   808.5'1   87-15600
ISBN: 0-517-56709-1
Book design by Dana Sloan
10 9 8 7 6 5 4 3 2 1
First Edition

Contents

Introduction

One of the worst cases of nervousness I ever witnessed was during my theatrical career as a singing actress. I was playing Lady Thiang, the head wife, in the original production of *The King and I* with Yul Brynner and Gertrude Lawrence, the great English star, who played Mrs. Anna.

Miss Lawrence was not really a singer. She was a "diseuse"—someone who half sings and half talks a song. She was unable to sustain a vocal line. She could get away with her diseuse style in most of the songs like "Shall We Dance?" and "Getting to Know You." But the song "Hello Young Lovers" defeated her nightly. It required a singer who could sustain tone. It was not a song that could be talked. Every night, just before Miss Lawrence had to sing it, the perspiration would break out on her forehead and flow down over her face like Niagara Falls.

Rodgers and Hammerstein called in psychiatrists to help her overcome her fear. That didn't work. She tried to conquer it by coming to the theater every day at about four o'clock, putting on her makeup and going out on stage to vocalize. This didn't help either. She continued to be tortured by fear of "Young Lovers" and never did overcome it. I vowed that one day I would find a cure for nervousness that would prevent this kind of suffering. And I did.

Almost Everyone Gets Nervous

Cuban leader Fidel Castro, known for his oratorial skill, has confessed, "I have stage fright. I don't like making speeches."

The governor of a western state, now a presidential hopeful, was taken to task by a local newspaper columnist for his nervousness on the campaign trail: "Your nervousness showed. Your speech was halting. Lots of 'ahs' like when the doctor looks down your throat, run-on sentences, swallowed words . . . too bad because the speech was substantive . . . forceful words a Mario Cuomo could use passionately were flat. No feeling, no pizzaz. I hope you can bring style up to the level of substance. With both, you might just make it."

Signs of nervousness are fatal to the careers of most politicians. Remember the perspiration on Richard Nixon's upper lip during the televised Nixon-Kennedy debates in the 1960 presidential campaign?

Willard Scott, the weatherman on the "Today" show, says he fights nervousness every single morning before going on the air.

Sir Laurence Olivier developed stage fright at the age of sixty. Every night his throat would dry up and he experienced all the symptoms of panic. He forbade any actor on the stage with him to look him in the eye. For six years, he was tormented by nervousness.

Comedienne Lily Tomlin, who's appeared in movies and television and nightly on Broadway, was so nervous about appearing on the televised Rockefeller Plaza Christmas tree-lighting ceremony that she held up the taping of the show for forty minutes and almost refused to go on at all.

The most profitable case of nervousness I dealt with was for two people at Ogilvy & Mather, the advertising agency. The chairman of the company called two of his vice presidents into his office one day to tell them they were going to have to give presentations at the annual meeting. The then chairman said, "You two get so nervous you make everyone watching you nervous. I wish I had somebody else to give the presentations but I don't, so you'll have to do them." One of them used to take Valium and a drink before presenting. It didn't make his presentation better. It only made him think it was better.

Just around that time, an article on my foolproof control of nervousness appeared in *Esquire* magazine. The two O&M executives read it and instantly called for an appointment. We worked together for a total of six hours. At the end of that time, I still wasn't satisfied. I said,

"Come back for one more hour on the house." After that hour I was satisfied that they'd licked nervousness.

They spoke at the annual meeting and the chairman was ecstatic. "You were great! What the devil happened to you two?"

"We went to see Dorothy Sarnoff," they replied.

"Go back and see if you can buy her," said he. "We were meant for each other." And that's how nervousness made Speech Dynamics a subsidiary of Ogilvy & Mather.

Preventing Nervousness

mental misery - butterflies - pounding heart - sweaty palms

I've introduced my foolproof mental and physical control of nervousness to more than seventy thousand people from all over the world: prime ministers, presidential candidates, governors, senators, ambassadors (I've been consultant to the U.S. State Department through four administrations), CEOs of the Fortune 500 top corporations, many psychiatrists, doctors, housewives, salesmen, bankers, college kids, authors, television personalities, newscasters, talk-show hosts and guests on all kinds of TV programs. Authority increases, book sales soar, Neilsen ratings and salaries go up, up and up.

You may remember the 1976 vice-presidential debate between Republican Robert Dole and Democrat Walter Mondale. That Robert Dole came across quite differently from the Robert Dole we see today.

News stories indicated:
- He wasn't mean but he looked mean.
- His style was a little on the arrogant and cynical side.
- His wit was acerbic.
- His expression often seemed to be a sneer in response to his opponent.
- He sank onto the lectern leaning heavily on one arm, and he talked over his shoulder.

It turned out that a director had told him to hide his World War II-crippled arm by leaning on it on the lectern. I pointed out that the side stance really called attention to the arm and that if he stood at the lectern straight shouldered, with upper torso held high, both hands on the lectern, we would not even notice his arm. He changed not only his physical bearing but his attitude as well, and consequently became the stronger, pleasant personality we know today. He also abandoned a less groomed look for well-cut suits, pastel shirts and natty ties. The presentation of Robert Dole was enhanced.

Joan Ganz Cooney, founder and president of the Children's Television Workshop, which produces "Sesame Street," and a member of the board of several large corporations, was terrified at the prospect of giving a commencement speech at Smith College in front of seven thousand people. She'd been trying to conquer nervousness since she was nineteen years old.

After three two-hour sessions working on her talk, on expressing joy and ease at the lectern and creating a strong presence and authority, Cooney delivered her commencement speech and got a standing ovation. No more nervousness.

*   *   *

Our foolproof system for the mental and physical control of nervousness has been taught to thousands of people who were told "If you do what we show you and it doesn't work, you get your money back." We've never had to return one dollar.

We have a file called "Luv Letters" from clients. Over and over again they say almost the same thing: "Thank you, you've been able to do for me in six hours what three years or six or ten years of analysis, therapy, hypnotism, or any other cure suggested to nervous mankind hasn't been able to do—prevent nervousness and give me self-confidence."

You, too, can learn to prevent nervousness. In this book are all the questions about nervousness and confidence I've been asked over the years. You'll get the answers, the solutions, the formulas that have miraculously cured so many thousands of people. You will keep cool in the hot seat and never be nervous again.

Questions I Ask My Clients

The first question I ask clients is, "What are you thinking of while waiting to give your talk or presentations?" The answers run something like these:

"Did I prepare enough?"

"What if I forget?"

"Should I have rehearsed more?"

"What if I'm a flop?"

"Why did I say I'd give this talk?"

"Oh, God, I wish it were over!"

Wonder and doubt! Wonder and doubt! Wonder and doubt are fear. Nervousness is caused by the fear of looking ridiculous to others. You will learn a foolproof method for presenting yourself, your ideas, your product in any communicating situation so you WON'T look ridiculous to others. Therefore you won't have the FEAR of looking ridiculous to others. No more wonder and doubt! If you want to skip right to "Antinervousness Control," turn to page 66. Then turn back here to get all the important information leading up to it.

The second question I ask clients is, "Who are the speakers you've heard in your lifetime who commanded and held your attention throughout as they spoke?"

Martin Luther King, Jr., Franklin Roosevelt, Winston Churchill and Mahatma Gandhi knew how to appeal strongly to their listeners. But the name that invariably goes to the top of everyone's list is John F. Kennedy.

Kennedy communicated joy and ease, credibility, authority and concern. He gave you the feeling that he was personally involved for your involvement and benefit. He seemed strongly committed for your sake.

Martin Luther King, Jr., communicated passion and touched people's souls. Reverend Jesse Jackson has passion too, but a different kind. After his address to the Democratic National Convention in July 1984, the *New York Times* reported: "Witnesses in the audience could see people weeping as Mr. Jackson rolled into his peroration. A white man in the North Carolina delegation fought back tears . . . Unless you had a heart of stone, Jesse Jackson had to reach you."

If you've ever heard British Labour Party leader Neil

Kinnock, he lifts you out of your seat. He has what I call "fire in the belly."

Mario Cuomo, governor of New York and presidential hopeful, moves audiences by personalizing his message. When he talked about his father with calluses on his hands working hard to make a better life for his family, you were moved. He was sending a message between the lines. "I learned from my father to work hard, and I'm working hard for the people of New York."

Going back in history, according to *New York Times* columnist John Russell, William Gladstone, several times prime minister of England in the nineteenth century, had no peer then or today as a public speaker. Gladstone in his late seventies "campaigned with no band, he had no amplification. He never painted his old face. He had no podium to hoist him high above the crowd, even when that crowd numbered in the thousands. . . . This old man spoke for an hour, and then for another hour, and yet another . . . Nobody coughed and nobody went home."

Four Positive Vibes That Make a Commanding Speaker

What are the "vibes" that commanding speakers give out?

The English poet John Milton said, "A good teacher is one whose spirit enters the soul of the pupil." For me, a good speaker is one whose spirit enters the soul of the listener. To enter the soul of your listener you need to communicate several important "vibes."

Vibe #1: Joy and Ease
If a singer goes for a high note and isn't totally confident when she begins the phrase, you feel her anxiety and it

makes you uncomfortable. If a speaker isn't comfortable, you feel uncomfortable listening to him. When the speaker is at ease and seems to enjoy presenting to you, you feel at ease. He's in control of himself and of you. So you listen.

Vibe #2: Sincerity, Credibility, Concern

I've worked with enough politicians to know that they must seem to be sincere to win the voter's confidence. Sincerity and credibility create instant trust.

James Burke, chairman of Johnson & Johnson, the pharmaceutical company, appearing on television after the Tylenol poisoning incident, reassured his stockholders and an entire nation that their investments and their safety were secure. He demonstrated the kind of leadership quality that tripled his company's profits during his nine-year tenure as chief executive. He came across totally sincere and credible and he also demonstrated the next most valuable quality—concern.

Elie Weisel, the Nobel laureate for literature, is one of the best communicators of sincerity and soul. He talks to your mind and your heart and holds you spellbound.

Vibe #3: Enthusiasm

The next time you visit your local department store, look around and see which cosmetic counter is the busiest.

You'll probably see more customers buying at the Clinique counter than any other. Although the women selling Revlon or Chanel or Yves Saint Laurent cosmetics may be more beautiful, the women at the Clinique counter rack up more sales at the cash register. They sell with "belief of product"—with passion.

Enthusiasm, energy, intensity (urgency for politi-

- Your ideas and the image and language in which you express them
- Tone
- Appearance
- Eyes
- Face

They give the power to:

- Make a strong impression
- Get the account
- Make the sale
- Win the case
- Hit pay dirt

The Six Steps of Intelligent Anticipation That Prevent Nervousness

1.
Preparation

Message Giver #1: Ideas, Image and Language

When should you start writing your talk or presentation?

So many people who are giants at their desks become pygmies at the lectern. They usually wait too long to write their talks. The memorable one-liners and moving phrases that go down in history don't come from last-minute bursts of inspiration. The most polished, smoothly delivered spontaneous-sounding talks are the result of many hours of long, hard work. Mario Cuomo started ten days before the convention and worked a total of sixteen hours to write his memorable keynote address for the 1984 Democratic convention.

Brenda Milner, a Canadian neurophysicist who's done ground-breaking work on the function of memory, spends entire afternoons composing a single sentence for her scientific presentations.

Begin preparing your talk at least three weeks ahead of time. "I haven't got the time!" you'll say. It's a constant

surprise to me the number of smart, high-powered executives who come to me to prepare an important talk they're
going to give and tell me apologetically, "I just wrote it"
or "I wrote it on the plane." They should know better.

If you don't have time to do yourself justice, don't
accept the speaking engagement. When I work at the
State Department, I give the diplomats an assignment and
they're so disciplined, they come in the next day with a
finished, well-written talk. Pressured as they are with day-
and-night international crises, they make the time to do
it, and they do it well.

What's the best way to prepare your talk?

A cartoon in *The New Yorker* showed a man standing at
the lectern saying, "And now I should like to depart from
my prepared text and speak as a human being."

Most talks written by speakers or by their speechwriters suffer from one common fault. They're put together in written, not spoken, language. A talk or
presentation whether to ten or a thousand people must be
spoken, not read or memorized.

If it's in spoken language on the page it's easier to
deliver conversationally. Write your talk with your tongue
as well as your pen. Use short sentences. (Mark Twain
advised writers to strike out every third word. "You have
no idea what vigor it adds to style," he said.) Use the
active voice—"I believe" rather than "It is believed."
Stick with contractions—*isn't, you're, it's*—and use pro-
nouns—*we, you, I.* Use lots of "you, your, we, our" instead of the third person impersonal. These make your
talk conversational.

Write the way you talk to someone sitting across the dinner table when you want to make a point. Talk it as you write it. You should be able to sound conversational the first time you speak it from the typewritten page.

Back up your generalizations with specifics—examples, statistics or facts. Supporting your points with evidence reinforces your message and contributes to your authority.

Let the ideas percolate in your head before you start writing. Think: What can I tell the listener that nobody's told him before in a way that nobody's spoken about it before.

Do your thinking anywhere—driving the car, cleaning up the kitchen, waiting for the elevator, walking to work. Ideas can be sleep thieves. They can keep you awake at night or distract you when you're working on something else. Keep a notebook with you—in your briefcase, purse, by your bedside, handy at all times to jot down your thoughts.

"Good writing," says Harvard historian Richard Marius, "is a kind of wrestling with thought." Begin the wrestling match early. Two days before your presentation is too late to go into the ring and come up with a winning idea.

How do you organize your talk?

There are three parts to your talk or presentation: the introduction, body and conclusion. Make a folder for each section and as you gather research, quotes, anecdotes, evidence, put the information into the appropriate folder.

Walter Wilson, a senior writer in the public affairs

department of Exxon, suggests you "boil your message down to three or four major points." Then write an outline. "An outline," says writer Eleanor Foa Dienstag, "is really a detailed road map of your original points. It forces you to examine the logic of your thinking before you're enmeshed in the subtler dilemmas of tone and style."

In *The Elements of Style,* the classic text for rules of good writing, William Strunk, Jr., and E. B. White stress the importance of developing your idea from a suitable design.

Write or type your first draft using double spacing. It gives you room between the lines for inserting additional thoughts and for applying the scissors for the cut-and-paste system of editing later on. As you write your draft, use the letters A and E to indicate where you think you'll need an anecdote or example in your talk.

What's a special recipe for a good talk on paper?

What the listener wants to hear, says *New York Times* columnist William Safire, is "words full of meaning—writing that binds thoughts together with a purpose."

You've read all the usual advice about this: think about the purpose of your talk, your audience, the occasion. But here are some questions William Safire uses to measure good writing:

> Does the talk contain new thoughts or a new way
> of looking at things?
> Does it say something worth saying in a personal
> manner?
> Is it structured?

Does it use well-turned phrases?
Does it move its listener to action?
Do its language and images dress up the ideas?
Can you feel its purpose?

Write for instant comprehension. "A flowery speech is a bad speech," says William Safire. Simple straight English prose can be used to build a great speech.

Don't use words you can't pronounce. One CEO used the words *legerdemain* and *prestidigitation* in a talk. He tripped over them. In rehearsing a Broadway musical, the author told me that if I stumbled over his words twice, he'd written them wrong for me.

Avoid using jargon—words that are pretentious or meaningless from overuse or obscure to anyone outside your profession.

> Objective consideration of contemporary phenomena compels the conclusion that success or failure in competitive activities exhibits no tendency to be commensurate with innate capacity, but that a considerable element of the unpredictable must invariably be taken into account.

George Orwell illustrated the confusion of jargon by first giving us this jargonized paragraph to contemplate. Then he gave us the simplified version of the ideas, quoting this passage from the King James version of the Bible.

> I returned and saw under the sun, that the race is not to the swift, nor the battle to the strong, neither yet bread to the wise, nor yet riches to men of

understanding, nor yet favor to men of skill, but time and chance happeneth to them all.

The first passage has thirty-eight words of ninety syllables. The original has forty-nine words, totaling only sixty syllables. The first passage doesn't have a single fresh, arresting phrase. And it doesn't convey even half the meaning of the original.

Use simple, widely understood words in place of technical terms, or important-sounding words, even for colleagues. Your listener will understand faster and he'll remember your message long after the jargon-riddled presentations have faded.

Strunk and White in *The Elements of Style* advise us to cut out "the leeches that infect the pond of prose, sucking the blood of words."

Don't rob yourself of authority. Use the English language well. Talk conversation language, not "literary" language. That's what John Kennedy did.

OASES

What's the best way to open?

Serve up your talk with color and flavor by using OASES —*Open* with something that's unpredictable; *Anecdote,* quotes; *Spoken Speech; Example* or *Evidence;* and a *Socko* or *Significant* finish. If you include these in your preparation, you won't be wondering about the content of your talk. That's one less reason to be nervous.

Never open with the usual "It's a pleasure," "It's a privilege . . . I'm delighted, . . ." etc. Always begin with the unexpected, the unpredictable, an instant attention getter:

A question:

"How many of you fly more than twenty thousand miles a year?"

A quotation:

"Teddy Roosevelt once said, 'Nine-tenths of wisdom consists of being wise in time.' "

An observation:

There's a sign at a country crossroads near Rutland, Vermont, that says, "Choose the right rut because you're going to be in it for seventeen miles."

Or just one word:

"Money!"

What do you think of opening with a joke to relax your audience and yourself?

Let me take the word *relax* apart:

    Re means away from

    Lax means discipline

    Relax = away from discipline

When you get up to give a talk you want to be totally disciplined, i.e., in control. If you want to tell a joke

- It must be to the point
- It must be told as succinctly as possible
- It must be timed so that the punch line will elicit a laugh
- It must be fresh. It's very important to make sure it hasn't been making the rounds lately.

I was at a luncheon where the president of a broadcast company began his talk with a familiar joke and I sensed a huge wave of embarrassment for him sweep over the audience.

But here's a joke that worked. A woman vice president of an engineering company used it to open a talk on strategic planning to a large management group:

> Recently a well-known Lakewood attorney was driving down the road—very pleased about his business, how successful he was, his big new house, his big new car.
>
> All of a sudden—*Wham*—a farmer coming out of the driveway on his tractor banged into him. The farmer was very upset. He jumped off his tractor and ran over to the car. The attorney was not feeling very good. The farmer ran back to his toolbox where he had a little bottle of Johnnie Walker. He ran back to the car and gave it to the attorney. He took a long drink and began to feel better.
>
> The farmer told him to drink a little more as he'd had a bad shock. So the attorney took a couple of big swigs. Now he's feeling very good. The farmer said, "Have some more." When the attorney asked the farmer to join him in finishing the bottle, the farmer said, "Oh, I couldn't do that, the police will be here any minute."
>
> Well, there's a message there. Obviously the farmer had done a little strategic planning. Maybe this plan doesn't qualify as a long-range business plan, but it was certainly carefully thought through.

There's a difference between humor and jokes. Humor can be leavening and communicate a sense of spontaneity.

24

Peter Desberg, professor at California State University, has studied the effects of humor and found that it speeds the assimilation of information.

Self-deprecating humor, humor pointed at yourself, almost always works—especially if you're up at the top of the corporate ladder. It puts the audience with you, not against you.

Israeli former prime minister of foreign affairs Abba Eban responded to a particularly effusive introduction by saying, "I thank you very much for those marvelous compliments. No politician can afford to be other than grateful for compliments, however undeserved. We receive them too rarely."

Greville Janner, a member of Britain's Parliament, writing in the English publication *Executive World,* included Eban's remarks along with several other politician jokes he uses in public speaking, among them:

A politician is a person who speaks while others sleep.

I once took some Americans to Westminster Abbey to show them the tomb of a deceased colleague. "Here lies a politician and an honest man," read the inscription. One American exclaimed, "I didn't know in Britain you buried two people in the same grave."

Here's a formula for humor that comedian Henny Youngman uses:

1. Use the joke or gag that fits your point and fits you. Give it a custom fit.
2. Personalize your stories. Name the characters and the place.

3. Laugh at yourself. Use yourself or your family as the butt of the joke. (Youngman always used his wife. Joan Rivers and Phyllis Diller used their husbands.)
4. Be brief. The mind cannot accept what the seat cannot endure.

What about the traditional advice to tell them what you're going to tell them, tell them, and tell them what you've told them?

Don't do it. It is old-fashioned and it's boring. It's also unnecessary, because if you give your message dynamically they'll remember what you told them.

Why is it important to use anecdotes?

If you tell me, I may listen. If you show me, I'll pay attention. If you involve me, I'll learn.

Anecdotes involve your listener. When you tell one, your listener sees a real scene. During one of my two-day seminars at the State Department, I worked with a deputy secretary for Latin American Affairs. The first day he gave a talk describing some of the horrors he'd witnessed in Central America. He said, "Thousands of innocent people are being killed every day." Can you picture in your mind's eye thousands of people being killed?

Compare this to the way he presented it the next day. "How would you feel if your doorbell rang, you opened the door, and there at your feet lay the body of your best friend?"

Anecdotes and quotes liven up your talk. You can

never have enough of them. Collect them greedily. Whenever I hear an anecdote my ears prick up. Recently Nancy Reagan said, "A woman is like a tea bag. You don't really know what she's like until she gets into hot water." I've filed that one away.

At a luncheon recently, the economic forecaster Leo Cherne was the speaker. His talk was loaded with good quotes. A management consultant I know was copying them all down to use in his talks. Political columnist George Will, it's rumored, calls an eccentric Englishman named Tom Dickinson for his anecdotes and quotes.

So keep your eyes and ears open for anecdotes and quotes that make a point. Get in the habit of collecting them when you read or hear them. Build up a quote and anecdote file—it'll pay off.

When do you use emotion?

Rarely does emotion belong in business presentations. It's great for charitable appeals and political campaigns. But be careful to control it. Edmund Muskie's tear on behalf of his wife during the 1972 presidential campaign was costly.

Emotion used simply goes straight to the soul. Elie Weisel used emotion in his Nobel prize acceptance speech. It was gripping to read; it must have been heart-rending to hear.

What's a good way to close your talk?

A closer is to a talk what a high note is to an aria. Its cadence should trigger applause.

Quotes can be excellent closers. Here's the closer of a talk to top management about planning for the future: "So let's take the advice of Ted Turner who said, 'Lead, follow, or get out of the way.'"

Here's a humorous close from a speech "Re-Skilling Britain" at the Annual Conference of The Institute of Directors, London, delivered by Jock Elliott, chairman emeritus of Ogilvy & Mather: "I know you'll be disappointed if I don't bring you up to date on my suit situation. You'll be glad to hear that I got a new suit. From a well-known tailor. Double breasted—the latest thing. I would have worn it today, but it's back in Savile Row. The sleeves were too short. Which is more than you can say about this speech. Thank you."

If you don't have a strong quote or a point-making anecdote to end with, use anaphora. Anaphora is the repetition of the same word or words at the opening of consecutive phrases.

> If we have a vision—
> If we all put our shoulders to the wheel—
> If we want our children to have a bright future—
> Then let's have the courage to act now.

Anaphora has a cadence and rhythm that signals to the audience you'll be coming to a stop the way a gear-shift car goes from third gear to second to first to stop. Applause, applause.

How long should most talks be?

Most talks should be no longer than twenty minutes, forty minutes maximum if you have a lot of information to communicate.

One hundred seventy words on the page equals one minute's talking time. That's in the North. (It's about 155 words per minute in the South, 160 per minute in Britain, 180 per minute in Italy and France.)

One hundred seventy words is about three-quarters of a typed, double-spaced manuscript page, or about one double-spaced handwritten page on an eight-by-eleven-inch ruled pad. A fifteen- or twenty-minute talk adds up to about ten to twelve typed manuscript pages.

How do you know if you have a good talk on paper?

"I can't write," all my clients say. You don't have to be Woody Allen or William Safire to write a good talk or presentation. Knowing your limitations can show you where to concentrate your efforts. The writer Somerset Maugham wrote in his autobiography that he knew he had "a limited vocabulary, no lyric quality, no gift for metaphor or simile, no imaginative sweep . . . I knew I should never write as well as I could wish, but I thought with pains I could arrive at writing as well as my natural defects allowed."

Be the best of yourself. Follow these guidelines, and your talk should sound like you. Go to the lectern or into your client's office without wondering, Is my material interesting? Persuasive? Now you can eliminate wonder and doubt about content.

What do you do if your boss gives you a bad speech to deliver?

Years ago I was asked to sing the role of Aida in *"My Darling Aida,"* a Broadway version of the Verdi opera.

29

The script was wonderful. Before the show went into re-hearsal, I went to Europe to do a USO tour for our troops stationed abroad. I did twenty-one shows in seventeen days.

When I got back to New York, I discovered the author had completely rewritten the script. He'd destroyed all the beauty and strength of the original character. I was heartbroken. I called my drama coach, Lina Abarbanel, who had played the original Merry Widow on Broadway. She was eighty-five years old and she'd coached me for every Broadway part I ever played. She taught me that lines could be poorly written but that the tone of your voice could convey meaning the words did not express. (Richard Burton could move you just by reading the telephone book.) And the way you held your body could portray a sense of the character more powerfully than lines.

When I told her what had happened to the Aida script, she told me, "Ignore the words. Pretend the script is written in Russian. You sing in foreign languages you don't understand but you color your delivery through tone. Convey the character and emotions you want in the Aida show by the way you color your tone."

I took her advice and got the reviews of a lifetime.

What can I do to get a speechwriter to write better for me?

Senator Barry Goldwater was interviewed recently on the "MacNeil/Lehrer News Hour." Jim Lehrer asked him, "When I followed you on the presidential campaign trail in sixty-four, you were great with the crowds—warm, spontaneous. But when you spoke on official occasions, you didn't come across as yourself. You came across as formal and reserved. What happened?"

"My speechwriters," said Goldwater. "I was stuck to the page. My natural speaking style is spoken speech but my speechwriters gave me talks that had to be read."

Professional speechwriters seem to forget to write in spoken language. A client of mine who's a speechwriter remembered how excited he was sitting in the back of a big auditorium, waiting to hear his boss deliver the first speech he ever wrote. "When he was finished," said my client, "I was humiliated. He read every word I wrote, but I realized I hadn't written it to be spoken. I'd written it to be read."

When I did a seminar at the State Department for speechwriters, I asked each one of them to go to the lectern and give the talks they'd written for their bosses. Not one of them could talk their speeches. The enemy: written language.

Not only does a speechwriter have to write in spoken language, but it has to fit his client's tongue. The president of a large communications company and a client of mine for many years called me the other day. After giving many successful talks he was suddenly having trouble. "I don't know what's happened," he said. He came to the office with the talk he was rehearsing. As soon as I looked at it, I knew what the problem was. He'd hired a new speechwriter who was writing words my client never used.

After the talk is written, what's the next step?

George Bernard Shaw wrote to a friend and apologized, "I'm sorry it's such a long letter, I didn't have time to write a short one."

31

It takes more work to write a short, tight talk or presentation than a long, rambling one. Talks are always too long in the first draft. "First drafts," says William Safire, "are usually stupid. Reject the notion that honesty and candor demand that you 'let it all hang out.' That's not honesty, that's intellectual laziness. Tuck some of it in, edit some of it out."

When George Shultz sent me his speech for a prayer breakfast with Ronald Reagan, his sentences were almost half a page long. I've never seen so many *and*s. They were like flyspecks on the page.

There's no talk that can't be improved by cutting, chopping, eliminating. Prune away the dead wood, the redundant, the rhetorical flourishes, anything that doesn't sound like you. Add what's missing. Make it tight, direct, to the point.

Don't fall in love with your own words. Be ruthless. Never use two words when one strong word will get the message across. Franklin D. Roosevelt knew how to pick the word that packed the wallop. When he asked Congress to declare war against Japan, his talk originally opened: "December 7, 1941. A day that will live in world history." In his own hand, Roosevelt crossed out "world history" and wrote in the word "infamy." And so great speeches are made stronger by careful editing.

Use the cut-and-paste system of editing. I cut out the section that doesn't belong and tape it to the right place. Don't worry if you end up with pages that look like ancient scrolls of hieroglyphics. Cut-and-paste jobs save valuable time. Of course, if you use a word processor, it will do the cutting and pasting for you.

When she was ambassador to the United Nations, Jeane Kirkpatrick used her friends to help her edit. At lunch one day, she asked me how I liked her talk at the Republican convention; she told me she wrote it herself. "After I edited a couple of drafts with my husband," she said, "we sat down and went over it with Norman Podhoretz [editor of *Commentary*] and his wife, Midge Decter. Then my husband and I edited it again. Next we talked it over with Irving Kristol and his wife. Then more editing and more rewriting. Last, it was the William Buckleys. Then the final rewrite and editing and lots of rehearsals. So, when I got up there to talk, I was speaking not as one voice, but as several voices."

David Ogilvy has another system. He sends copies of his talks to friends saying, "Improve Please." His friends say he doesn't often accept their suggestions, but they like being asked.

After your first edit, put your draft away and don't look at it for a few days. When you go back to it, you'll see much more clearly what needs to be tightened and weeded out.

When I have the final version, what next?

When your talk is close to final, talk it into a tape recorder. Then play it back. Listen to it with your back to the cassette player. When you're facing it, you're subjective. With your back to it, you listen objectively. Don't pay any attention to your delivery—not yet. That comes later.

You'll hear right away if your talk is written in spoken speech. Listen for content. You'll know what's missing, or what there's too much of. Listening always percolates new ideas for me. Re-edit your talk and record it again until you're satisfied.

Editing puts the polish and shine on your talk and makes it easier to deliver.

REMEMBER

Organize your material.
Write in spoken speech.
Start with a catchy opening.
End with a socko finish. Use anecdotes and quotes.
Strengthen with several edits.

Message Giver #2: Appearance

How important is appearance when making presentations?

It was said of Charles de Gaulle, the French statesman, that the ambiance of a room changed when he entered. Why does a good actor command your attention when he comes onstage, even before he opens his mouth to speak? Because he has the magic of *presence*.

Presence is created quite simply by bearing, the way you carry yourself that says, Stop, Look, Listen. "People with presence are naturally in control of any social situation," says psychologist Richard Boyatzis, president of the McBer Research Group, which is studying the skills that enable a person to persuade others to his vision. "These people are very secure about themselves." He points to the example of the character Hawkeye Pierce, played by Alan Alda in the television series "MASH," who was unflappable in even the most extreme crises. "That's the kind of confidence you need to use your social talents with brilliance."

Some people are born with presence. The rest of us have to create it. How? Simple. It's really more physical than psychological. If you play tennis, what happens to the muscles in your body in a serve at the moment of impact of racquet to ball? They contract and create tension, not tenseness, generating the power to smash the ball over the net. Use that same kind of "serve" tension when you "serve" yourself up at the lectern.

Try this at home. Stand in front of a mirror. Look at the way you're standing. Does it say Presence? Now stand with your weight evenly distributed on the balls of both feet. Carry your rib cage high and contract your stomach muscles. How do you look now? You automatically stand taller and straighter. This gives you the look of authority. It's not military posture, it's the bearing of confidence.

So many people sit in important meetings in what I call the Great American Meeting Position—a crescent moon—lounging back in the chair, legs out in front, total muscle collapse. They look passive, uninvolved, sort of idling in neutral.

Even when you're listening at a meeting you're being observed. You look alert and involved at meetings if you sit with rib cage held high, inclined slightly forward. If you're at a table modify your mother's adage: "Willie, Willie, if you're able, keep your elbows off the table." Put your forearms on the table, resting them on the table edge midway between your wrist and your elbow, your hands clasped (not fidgeting). This gives you the look of authority at a conference or panel.

Warren Christopher, deputy secretary of state for President Carter, was to appear on "Meet the Press" to be grilled about the Iran hostage crisis. I went down to Washington the day before to prepare him. He sat at the table, his body almost completely concave, his hands folded on the edge of the table like a schoolboy at his desk. This was not the look for dealing with an international crisis. As soon as he sat in the "authority" position —stomach muscles contracted, forearms resting on the edge of the table, hands clasped, he immediately looked like the person in command. Body Tension for Attention.

How important is the visual impact you make on your listener?

After I'd finished a talk for the Young Presidents' Organization University, the president, a CEO of a large corporation, went to the lectern to thank me. He was lounging on the podium, moving the mike around as though he were watering flowers. I went over to him, stood him up straight without the support of the lectern, buttoned his jacket, brushed his hair to the side, then handed him back the microphone.

The audience went wild. "Jack, you never looked better," they shouted. "Why don't you look like that all the time."

You can look like that all the time. Go to the lectern, make a presentation, sell your idea, product or service nervousness-free knowing you have the look of authority.

Message Giver #3: Tone

How should you sound at the lectern?

Conversational!

Unless you're an Abba Eban, who's the golden-tongued orator of our day, don't use a formal "speechmaking" style to deliver your talk. You want to talk *with*—not *at*—your listener.

When speaking to an audience, use the tone you'd use talking to someone sitting across the table from you at a dinner party when you want to persuade him to adopt your point of view.

I have a round table in my dining room that seats ten. Round tables encourage conversation. You don't get a crick in your neck from turning your head sideways to talk to the person sitting next to you. You can talk to the people beside you, across from you, kitty corner from you.

The editor of a successful magazine and her husband invited us to a dinner party. They set up five small round tables. They'd done everything to create a warm, comfortable environment.

But unfortunately the flower centerpieces were about three feet tall. You couldn't see the people sitting across from you, and you certainly couldn't talk with them. It reminded me of an old *New Yorker* cartoon of people sitting at just such a dinner table with an elaborate sprawling centerpiece, talking to each other across the table by telephone.

The first round table was made of petrified wood. King Arthur, the legend goes, used a round table as a way of giving all his knights equal status. The common shape for a dining table in the Middle Ages was a rectangle. People sat along one side of the table. The host sat in the middle, in front of the salt cellar, and honored guests "worth their salt" sat to his right, above the salt. Less important guests sat below the salt. The only way people could talk to each other was to shout.

The rectangle is the shape of tables in most corporate boardrooms. The biggest corporate conference table I ever saw was while giving a seminar at Rothschilds' in

London. It was about five feet across and fifteen feet long. Another football-field-size conference table is in the New York Stock Exchange boardroom. At these oversize tables, you don't have conversations—you talk at each other, not with each other.

The Dining Table Tone is the tone my dinner guests use when they're sitting at my round table over coffee and one is trying to persuade another to adopt his idea or cause. He says, "But, John, unless we do this, we're doomed to fail." As he speaks, he leans toward his listener, looks straight into his eyes, and talks with conviction, energy, passion.

That's the energy vibe he's sending out, the quality that infects the listener with belief in the idea. That's the tone for the lectern, the business presentation, the sales pitch, the campaign trail, whenever and wherever you speak in public.

What effect does this tone have on your listener? We hear about the mind's power to influence the body. But what about the power of the body to influence the mind? Imagine how your body responds to certain auditory stimuli. You recoil mentally as well as physically at the sound of chalk squeaking on a blackboard or a jackhammer cutting into cement. Contrast that reaction to the way the mind responds to the sound of the cello. Ahhhhh, says the mind, more.

Putting energy and resonance into your voice has a positive effect on the listener's body. The body urges the mind to say yes. If your voice is timid or quivers with nervousness, you sense it, the listener hears it, and you see his discomfort in his eyes. With energy in your voice, the listener says ahhhh, more. You read approval.

Message Giver #4: Eyes

Where should I be looking when I'm giving a talk?

In his July 6, 1987, editorial in *Newsweek* magazine George Will wrote, "We need politicians who look up from their texts. American audiences should be offended when a speaker proceeds to read to them. We know candidates can read. Almost all of them are always reading what staffers have written for them. They should quit reading at us."

Ralph Waldo Emerson said, "Eyes can threaten like a loaded pistol, insult like a hiss or kick, or by beams of kindness make the heart dance with joy."

Eyes are the first place you look when you meet someone for the first time. Eyes communicate volumes. Four hundred muscles go into composing the look in your eye.

"The eye shows the very spirit in visible form. In every different state of mind it assumes a different appearance. Joy brightens and opens it, grief half closes it and drowns it in tears. Hatred and anger flash from it like lightning. Love darts from it in the glances like the orient beam. Jealousy and squinting envy mark their contagious blasts from the eye. Devotion raises it to the skies" (*The Art of Speaking,* 1770).

During the Senate Watergate wiretapping inquiry, Henry Kissinger testified before the committee and gave himself away with his eyes. Kissinger seldom blinks. When he was asked a compromising question, one eye suddenly went *blink* and in an instant he lost credibility.

If your eyes aren't up as you talk, you won't get and hold attention. "Nobody buys from lidded eyes." Eyes should be up, looking at your listener, 90 percent of the time.

Try this with a friend. Ask her to say three sentences to you. What were her eyes doing while she was talking to you? Did she look directly into your eyes? Or did she look over at the wall, or the ceiling or down at her hands for her next thought?

As she talked to you, she was probably looking into only one of your eyes. Now you talk to her. Try to look into both of her eyes at the same time. It's impossible. You go cross-eyed.

From studying President Kennedy's television interviews, I learned something that's been invaluable to clients. As Kennedy spoke to the interviewer, he would look from one eye to the other—not with the swinging regularity of a clock pendulum, but as though he were planting his message into each eye. What came across to the listener was sincerity, and a reach for the soul.

By using eyes that way, you vary the amount of white showing in each eye. This makes eyes sparkle. Try that with your friend. Look at her, and talk from one eye to the other eye and back again—eye to eye to eye. . . . Ask her to do the same thing for you. See how much more lively her face looks while she's talking to you. And how much more deeply she touches you.

The chairman of the medical department of Mt. Sinai Medical School recently invited me to speak to his 350 second-year medical students about how to communicate with patients. I know and you know, doctors rarely look their patients in the eye. They'll straighten their desks, and they answer phone calls, make notes on a pad, do anything but focus on you. I told the students, "You've got to treat with soul. The patient must feel that at that moment in that room he's the only person in the universe for you."

Then I showed them the eye-to-eye-to-eye action. When they saw in each other what it did for touching soul, they said, WOW. The chairman said, "This is the most important thing these kids can start off with." Then he said, "The next thing you've got to do is teach this to the doctors and the professors, because they all talk with absent eyes."

Where do you look when you're talking to a large group?

There's so much bad advice about this: "Pick out a friendly face and talk to him," some experts say. "Talk to their noses," says another, or "Talk over their heads to the back of the room." Wrong!

You want to be 90 percent eyes-up during your talk. But up isn't enough. You want to eye sweep as you talk. What's eye sweeping? It's a slow continuous sweep with your eyes from one side of the room to the other, as though you were embracing the audience with your eyes.

It works like this: Glance down at your notes, pick up a phrase, then eyes up and sweep them across the audience, glance down, eyes up and sweep . . . phrase by phrase.

Make certain your eyes don't pass over your listener. They must "click" with every pair of eyes in the room— that is, as far back as you can see your listener. What do I mean by "click"? When you pass an attractive member of the opposite sex on the street, what happens? Your eyes click, they register the other's presence. They give or receive a message.

This click gives your listeners the feeling you're relating to each one of them individually. Even though they may be sitting in the back of the room and can't really see your eyes, they will read your intention for the deed. Eye sweeping creates the rhythm of listener attention. The listener knows your eyes will come back to him, so his attention is on you for the next eye pass. You focus on the listener, he focuses on you. Rewarded with your listener's attention, you know you're in control.

The wife of the president of an air-conditioning company brought her husband to me because he was such a bad speaker, never communicating with his listeners because he never looked at them. As soon as he used my method for eye talking, he became a splendid presenter. When he came for his last appointment, his wife came with him. She said she wanted to thank me. For the first time her children were seeing their father's eyes when he talked to them at the dinner table.

Here was a man who'd come to learn how to make stronger presentations for his company, but his family also reaped the benefits.

Message Giver #5: Face

Should I smile when I give a talk?

Have you ever noticed how many CEOs and presidents of corporations appear in public with their faces in "executive neutral," communicating absolutely nothing? The listener is distracted by this noncommunicating face and responds in kind.

The face you give the listener is the face you'll get looking back at you. If you animate your face, you're more likely to see animated listeners. Animation is the greatest cosmetic you can use, and it doesn't cost a cent. Animation is energy in the face. The message it gives the listener is: I'm glad I'm here, I'm glad you're here.

There's a difference between animation and "smile." "Smile" makes you look insipid. A smile can turn into a grin the way it did with Jimmy Carter.

Animation involves the whole face. It's action that comes not only through the eyes, but around the mouth and the whole face. It tells the listener you're at ease and glad to be right where you are—at the lectern, around a conference table or across a desk.

New research shows that the expression on your face also can influence the way *you* feel. At Allegheny College, researcher Patricia Ruselli recruited volunteer subjects to watch a sad slide presentation. She told half the subjects to frown while they watched it, the other half not to frown.

When the slide show was over, Ruselli reported, the frowners felt sadder than the nonfrowners, and their depression lasted for a few hours. What does this mean? It may mean that the brain receives sensory information from facial muscles and skin. Our faces may be telling us what to feel instead of being the reflection of our feelings.

So put "love apples"—that's what I call the little mounds around your cheekbones—into your cheeks and get two benefits for the one action. You'll show joy and ease, and the face you'll get looking back at you from the audience will say, "I'm glad you're here."

How can I use "love apples" in a challenging or hostile situation?

Your face can be a powerful weapon for deflecting hostility—from an audience, an interviewer, an employer. During the Nixon administration, I prepared people in the State Department for their meetings with Henry Kissinger when he was secretary of state. Kissinger seemed to intimidate many people. If members of his staff went into his office looking nervous, he'd probably be inclined to intimidate them. I suggested they go in wearing a benevolent face. A benevolent face says, I understand. It conveys a message of good will or positive expectation. It works. If you're going to be interviewed by Sam Donaldson, don't leave home without it.

If I use all five message givers, will I persuade my listener?

In a seminar I taught recently in Toronto, the president of a research firm told me that persuasion is: 8 percent content, 42 percent appearance, and a whopping 50 percent is how you say it. You ask, only 8 percent content? Well, 8 percent seems to be enough for politicians. Voters react more to image and style than to content. But what about a business presentation? Does content really count for so little? Say, two people are competing for a customer's business. The content of their presentations is equally good. Who makes the sale? The one with presence and the four vibes.

At lunch the other day I asked the CEO of a large

corporation what he looks for in a presentation. "I'm tired of being overvisualed," he said. "I look for the chemistry." A poll of clients choosing ad agencies in *Advertising Age* magazine agrees. A large number of clients said they chose the presentation team that showed enthusiasm and energy.

How do I know how I come across when I give a talk?

"One must try to observe oneself more and more objectively, to look at everything in oneself as though in another person," said Sigmund Freud.

The best way to see yourself objectively is on camera. I've been using a camera in my seminars since I started my Speech Dynamics business in a salon at the Hotel St. Moritz in 1966. I got the idea from my father. He was a surgeon and professor of anatomy. He was one of the first in his profession to take a camera into the operating room to film surgical techniques. He produced over six hundred educational films for Bell & Howell.

I remember watching those films as a child, especially the Before and After films of people whose faces he'd improved through plastic surgery. Those Before and After images made such an impression on me that I adopted the idea for my clients twenty years ago. Our Before and After videotapes show almost miraculous changes in just twenty-four hours.

Try to get hold of a video camera. If you don't have one, maybe you can rent one for the weekend or borrow one from a friend. Get someone to be cameraman. Give a four-minute talk to a make-believe audience. This is your

Before picture. The camera will show you an image of yourself as others see you. Once you see yourself on the playback, you'll see your strengths and weaknesses. I want you to keep your strengths, and I'll show you how to discard your weaknesses.

When you get to the end of the book, make another tape. This will be your After picture. You'll compare the two and I think you'll rejoice in the changes you see in yourself.

REMEMBER

The four vibes of a commanding speaker:

Joy and ease
Sincerity, credibility and concern
Enthusiasm, energy, intensity
Authority

The five message givers:

Ideas, image and language
Appearance
Tone
Eyes
Face

What questions should you ask the program organizer when you're invited to speak?

Who is the audience?
When I accepted an invitation to talk to the American Women in Economic Development at the Sheraton Hotel,

I asked who the audience was. It was a group of successful businesswomen in their thirties and forties. My opening line was, "When I found out who the audience was going to be today, I sent my blouse out to have an extra pair of shoulder pads put in it." Knowing who your audience is allows you to tailor your presentation to suit them.

Give your listeners something—an image or idea that has take-home value for them.

How many people will be there?
Knowing how many people are going to be listening to your talk helps you prepare to reach out to them and spares you last-minute surprises. When I went to Acapulco to talk to the American Society of Travel Agents, if I hadn't asked ahead of time, I'd have been overwhelmed to find myself standing at the lectern facing several thousand people.

My presentation was just as warm and personal as it would have been if I were talking to an audience of ten or fifteen. Two big airline executives who went before me presented very formally with expensive visual aids and twelve video screens at work. Despite their sophisticated multimedia effects, I was fortunate to get the highest rating from the audience. I think it was because I spoke *with* the audience, not at them.

Who else is speaking on the program? What will they be talking about?
I once attended a fund-raising appeal where the speaker had arrived to discover he was the sole entertainment— for an entire hour. He'd only prepared a twenty-minute presentation. Fortunately, he was quick on his feet and

saved himself by filling the remaining time with questions and answers.

William Paley, chairman of CBS, followed Harry Gray, the CEO of United Nuclear, as a speaker on an evening program. When Gray was finished, Paley stood up and gave exactly the same talk on exactly the same topic.

While Gray was talking, Paley should have used Gray's speaking time to make changes in his talk. Or he could have done as someone I know did in that situation. He got up and said, "I want to thank Mr. Smith for giving my talk for me. I have only a few comments to add." The audience would have appreciated it because by the time Paley spoke it was already 11:30, much too late for any dinner speaker to give a long talk.

What is the order of appearance?
If you have a choice, go first. The audience is fresh, alert, you get first licks at the program topic, and you can't suffer by comparison with a previous, stronger speaker.

The grandson of General Johnson, founder of the Johnson & Johnson Company, came to me with a speech he was preparing to christen a new hospital with the Johnson name in New Brunswick, New Jersey. He was concerned because he was going to follow James Burke, CEO of J & J and a former client of mine who is a riveting and persuasive speaker.

Bob had no experience at all speaking in public. "How can I get the audience to listen to me?" he asked. I said, "Bob, you're going to get up there and hold your own."

We rewrote his talk with OASES (see page 22). We rehearsed him four times aloud as though he were presenting in the real-life situation; he put the total mental

48

Those are the first things that will grab your attention and distract you when you glance down for your next sentence. Searching for a word on your page, says the writer Herman Wouk, is like standing at the front door of your house looking through all your pockets for the key to the front door. You may never find it.

Your notes should be your friend and give you confidence. What you need for the lectern is our fast food for the eyes—a script designed for the lectern that directs you quickly to where you pick up your next sentence.

This is the way your notes should look, at the lectern, the conference table, in your client's office.

1. GOOD MORNING YOU LOOK LIKE A GROUP OF WORLD TRAVELERS

2. DO YOU SPEND A LOT OF TIME IN THE AIR FOR BUSINESS OR PLEASURE?

3. AND DO YOU USUALLY ARRIVE AT YOUR DESTINATION BEFOGGED . . . BENUMBED . . . AND BEWILDERED—A VICTIM OF JET LAG?

4. YOU DON'T HAVE TO.

5. YOU CAN END A LONG FLIGHT FEELING JUST AS GOOD AS YOU STARTED IT.

6. YOU CAN FLY TO PARIS . . . OR CAIRO . . . OR TOKYO AND FEEL JUST AS FIT AS IF YOU'D GOTTEN AN 8-HOUR SLEEP IN YOUR OWN BED.

7. WHAT'S THE MAGIC?

8. IT'S CALLED THE JET LAG DIET. IT'S A REGIMEN DEVELOPED BY SCIENTISTS AT THE UNIVERSITY OF CHICAGO.

How do I convert my script to fast food for the eyes?

Talk your talk out loud. Wherever you think there's a pause or break in a sentence, pencil in a slash mark. Do this all the way through your text. Now your talk is broken down into phrases.

With a black felt-tip pen on a white lined pad, write each phrase in capital letters, beginning at the left-hand margin. Make the letters about half an inch high. Pair the phrases or group them by idea. Leave a double space between each group of phrases, and number each group on the left.

I hit upon this idea when I was working in the theater. I saw Bob Hope filming a show in Madison Square Garden and he used cue cards written out this way—large black capital letters on big pieces of white cardboard. The cards were placed strategically around the stage. Hope read from these cards but he gave the impression he was speaking spontaneously.

I modified the idea for my clients' speech script and called it Phrase-A-Line. It's my system for writing out a talk so that it becomes fast food for the eyes. I never give a talk without it, and I've given about fourteen hundred talks. It's my friend on the lectern. It feeds you phrases so that you can be 90 percent eye to eye with the audience.

With Phrase-A-Line on the lectern, you'll find it's easy to glance down, pick up your next phrase, and be eyes up and eye sweeping when you deliver it. Your left forefinger runs down the page by number as you talk, marking your place. No more scrambling for your next sentence or getting lost in a jungle of words. You'll know where you are, every minute.

The Oxford University Press uses this phrasing system

for the *Washburn College Holy Bible* they published in 1979. Called the "Modern Phrased Edition," the King James text is written like this for easy reading and voice coloring:

A PSALM OF DAVID

23:1 THE LORD IS MY SHEPHERD;
I SHALL NOT WANT.

2 HE MAKETH ME TO LIE DOWN IN GREEN
PASTURES;
HE LEADETH ME BESIDE THE STILL
WATERS.

3 HE RESTORETH MY SOUL;
HE LEADETH ME IN THE PATHS OF
RIGHTEOUSNESS
FOR HIS NAME'S SAKE.

4 YEA, THOUGH I WALK THROUGH THE
VALLEY OF THE SHADOW OF DEATH,
I WILL FEAR NO EVIL:
FOR THOU ART WITH ME;
THY ROD AND THY STAFF
THEY COMFORT ME.

5 THOU PREPAREST A TABLE BEFORE ME
IN THE PRESENCE OF MINE ENEMIES
THOU ANOINTEST MY HEAD WITH OIL;
MY CUP RUNNETH OVER.

6 SURELY GOODNESS AND MERCY SHALL
FOLLOW ME
ALL THE DAYS OF MY LIFE;
AND I WILL DWELL IN THE HOUSE OF THE
LORD
FOREVER.

TO THE CHIEF MUSICIAN
A PSALM OF DAVID

19:1 THE HEAVENS DECLARE THE GLORY OF
GOD;
AND THE FIRMAMENT SHEWETH HIS
HANDIWORK.

2 DAY UNTO DAY UTTERETH SPEECH, AND
NIGHT UNTO NIGHT SHEWETH KNOWL-
EDGE.

3 THERE IS NO SPEECH NOR LANGUAGE,
WHERE THEIR VOICE IS NOT HEARD.

4 THEIR LINE IS GONE OUT THROUGH ALL
THE EARTH,
AND THEIR WORDS TO THE END OF THE
WORLD,
IN THEM HE HAS SET A TABERNACLE FOR
THE SUN.

Phrase-A-Line is a boon to dyslexics. The prime minister of a foreign country came to me to work on an important talk. When I asked him to read it for me, he
confessed that he couldn't read. I said, "How do you give
a speech?" He said, "I have an aide who stands at my
elbow and reads it to me—then I memorize it." He didn't
know he had dyslexia. We tried Phrase-A-Line and for
the first time he was able to read his talk from the page.

I had another dyslexic client who was desperately
afraid to lift his eyes from the page for fear he'd lose his
place and never find it again. With Phrase-A-Line, he
could keep his eyes up 90 percent of the time.

Phrase-A-Line helps people with speech problems too.
The head of a large real-estate firm stuttered whenever
he came to a number. I had him spell out numbers as

words in Phrase-A-Line and he read them without a stutter.

As you familiarize yourself with your talk, you'll discover that you're retaining the design of the phrases on the screen of your mind. Your ear should capture by cadence the sound of the phrases as you talk them. And you will remember them.

After translating your first few talks into Phrase-A-Line you'll get used to thinking and writing talks in phrases. It cuts your writing time in half.

Talking from cue words on a page or index card works for some people. But cue words don't give you the momentum that phrases do. And what happens to your eyes when you're delivering from cue words? You might be eyes up, but you're not "clicking" with the audience. Instead of looking outward, controlling your listener, your eyes are focused inward as you try to remember what comes next. You're going to be "ahhing" while you're groping for your thought, and that loses you momentum.

When you've finished writing your talk in Phrase-A-Line, don't staple or paperclip the pages together. At the lectern, you want to be able to slide each page noiselessly aside as you finish it.

To make it easier to go on to the next page, I always dog-ear the lower right corner of each page. I bend the paper up a little so that it's easy to get hold of without looking at it. If you're talking eyes up, your audience won't even notice you're turning pages.

REMEMBER

Use Phrase-A-Line:
   Break your talk into phrases.

Print in large caps with a black felt tip on a white
   pad.

Make sure there are no blots and cross-outs.

Group phrases in pairs or threes, and number each
   group.

Dog-ear each page for easy turning.

2.
Rehearsing: How to Rehearse Like a Pro

Does silent rehearsing work?

I learned early on in my singing career that if I rehearsed my arias by mumbling them quietly under my breath I remembered them more easily. I rehearsed thirteen operas that way on the subway riding to and from rehearsals.

Research shows that vocalizing material out loud or mumbling it quietly under your breath helps you retain information. An experiment, done by Arthur Whimbey and Jack Lochhead at Xavier University in New Orleans, showed that students who voiced out loud the material they were studying learned and retained more information than those who didn't.

When Whimbey introduced his vocalizing method in a prefreshman program, many of his students jumped two grade levels in comprehension and increased their college aptitude scores by 14 percent. "Good learners vocalize," sums up Whimbey.

How should you rehearse your talk?

When I went to my first rehearsal of one of my Broadway plays, I was dismayed to find out that all the other actors had memorized their parts and I hadn't. I apologized to the director. He told me something I've never forgotten. He said, "Don't memorize, familiarize. Talk your lines four times aloud and you own them."

Take the word *rehearse,* and cross out the last two letters. What do you have? *Rehear.* When you "rehear" your text four times aloud, you make it yours. That's familiarizing. When you own your text, you control it. Your talk sounds spontaneous, not memorized.

Say your talk four times aloud as though in the real-life situation—standing on your feet, seeing the most skeptical of faces in front of you—and you own it.

If I say my talk four times aloud, will I remember it?

Yes, two steps help you remember your talk. First, you capture the phrase visually. Stamp it on the screen of your mind.

Second, you capture through cadence. Your ear captures the rhythm and sound of each phrase.

When you ask Information for a telephone number and you don't have a pencil handy, how do you remember it? You capture the cadence of the phrasing of the numbers: 555 - 2637—and repeat it while you're waiting to dial. You capture by cadence.

Capture by design visually
Capture by cadence orally

How do you keep your eyes up as you talk?

The phrase on the page dictates the phrasing for the eyes and the tongue. If you've rehearsed four times, your text should look familiar to you now so you can be eyes-up 90 percent of the time. Eyes up on all openings and closings, ends of questions, warnings, exhortations. Reward listener attention.

How much rehearsal do you need to sound sponta-neous and feel confident?

Boardroom Reports, a newsletter for top-level managers, recently printed some bad advice about this. "Rehears-ing," said the newsletter, "is usually not recommended. . . . Unrehearsed presentations have the advantage of freshness and spontaneity which only comes from thought uttered the first time."

This is nonsense. The way to sound spontaneous is to rehearse. And not just once. Too many executives think that all they need to do before giving a talk or presenta-tion is to go over it on the airplane on the way to their speaking engagement. You won't sound spontaneous, you'll just sound unprepared.

If the Greek orator Demosthenes had felt the same

way about rehearsing, he never would have become his nation's most persuasive statesman. For three months, Demosthenes shut himself up in an underground study to learn the skills of oratory. To make sure he didn't come out until he'd achieved his goal, he shaved off the hair on one side of his head. When the hair grew back, Demosthenes came out of his cave, an accomplished orator.

As long ago as 1770, the author of *The Art of Speaking* took public speakers to task for not giving rehearsal more importance:

> Actors rehearse and practice over and over many a time before they ever appear in public. But there are, I believe, no other public speakers among us who take such pains, although they bestow great pains in improving themselves in learning, which shows that the neglect of this accomplishment is more owing to a due sense of its usefulness than to any other cause.

You don't have to go underground for three months like Demosthenes to prepare your talk. But to command and hold attention at the lectern, and be free of nervousness —rehearse four times aloud.

How close to the time I deliver my talk should my last rehearsal be?

As close to delivery time as possible. If your talk's at 9:00 A.M., get up at 6:00 to rehearse and your page will be a friend on the lectern.

A page left unrehearsed from the day before goes ice

cold on the lectern. A page rehearsed just before you go on is fast food for the eyes.

So many executives tell me they can't spend the time to rehearse. My answer is, if you can't spend the time, don't accept the speaking engagement. Jock Elliott, chairman emeritus of Ogilvy & Mather, takes twenty-eight hours to prepare a talk. He finds the time and it pays off. He's one of the best speakers I know.

Triumph Through Tone

How important is the sound of the voice?

The late columnist Eugenia Sheppard said of advertising executive Mary Wells Lawrence, "Her low, thrilling voice makes the maddest ideas seem perfectly possible."

And who can ever forget that cellolike voice of Representative Barbara Jordan during the House Judicial Committee's Nixon impeachment hearings. It was low, rich, mellow, and she spoke in flowing phrases.

Just as the mind influences the body, so the body influences the mind. A shrill, nasal voice can have the same effect on your listener as chalk screeching on the blackboard. But the voice with overtones and chest resonance soothes and strokes the body and mind the way a cello does.

One day Frank Sinatra's secretary called to make an appointment for his wife Barbara. He didn't like the sound of her voice. She's beautiful, but her voice didn't match her looks. It was too high, too "little girl."

Barbara Sinatra often stood in for her husband to accept awards at dinners that he didn't want to attend. The writing of her talk was as "little girl" as her voice—very cutesy-pooh. We changed it so that it was more womanly, and lowered her voice, exchanging nasal resonance for chest resonance. Then she sounded as lovely as she looked.

Recently a Japanese woman came to learn how to be more assertive in sales pitches. You'd never have believed she was a successful free-lance graphics designer, for she sounded like a shy little girl.

She explained that in Japan, a woman who speaks forcefully is considered brash and aggressive. I pointed out she wasn't wearing a kimono, but she was using a kimono voice. She had her own company; she was presenting herself to clients every day. She couldn't be subservient and gentle, but she shouldn't be aggressive; she should sound pleasantly assertive.

She got rid of her whisper voice and talked so that she could hear the overtones of her voice in her own ear. No more tiptoe kimono sound. I put her in one of my two-day group seminars to teach her to project when presenting to a group, and she blossomed. Her gorgeous alabaster face was animated and that lit up her dark eyes. It was a completely different packaging.

I think Jackie Onassis has two voices. I sat next to her at the St. Moritz fountain once and she didn't order her chocolate sundae in her public little-girl voice.

How can I make my voice more appealing?

To find out how you sound to others, record your talk after you've rehearsed it four times out loud. Play it back and this time listen for your delivery. The voice that sells best projects with energy and varies the pacing and phrasing, and uses pauses for effect.

For voice projection, put your hand on your abdominal muscles where the ribs splay. Contract these muscles the way you would when rowing a boat. Pretend you're pulling back the oars. The muscles contract on each pull of the oars, pulling back and up. Now exhale on an *s* sound while you're contracting your muscles. Make a long hissing sound. Use those muscles in contraction to support your voice.

Chest resonance is enhancing. Nasal resonance is irritating. If you think your voice is nasal and want to get rid of the nasality, put one hand on your abdominal muscles, the other hand flat on your chest. That hand should feel vibrations on your chest bone as you speak. Try this: say *low, low, low* and see if you can feel chest resonance. Practice over and over, until you do, and you can acquire a more attractive voice in one day.

When the telephone rings, it's a good idea to say *low low low* before you pick it up. Say your hello in the second *low*. Most people pick up the telephone with a high, questioning hello. The hello in the second *low* has warmth to it. The person on the other end feels right away he has a friend.

Is the voice important in selling my idea, product or service?

In a cold, unheated room a critic listening to a friend reading from a talk he was preparing cried out in desperation, "My dear friend, either put fire in your words, or your words in the fire, or I shall not be able to stay here a minute longer."

A well-written talk doesn't compensate for a monotonous delivery. "Monotony," explains *The Art of Speaking,* "is holding one uniform humming sound through the whole discourse, not rising or falling."

Most people think that to emphasize you speak more loudly or more vehemently. Or jump on one word or go up in pitch. Cicero, the Greek orator, warned public speakers as long ago as 44 B.C. to "remit from time to time somewhat of the vehemence of his speaking and not utter every passage with all the force he can. To set off more strongly the more emphatic parts, do as the painters by means of shades properly placed make the figures stand off bolder."

Most of us who took public-speaking classes were taught to go up in pitch for emphasis. Wrong. To emphasize a word or phrase, go down in pitch . . . "an extraordinary talent." Lower your pitch on both words and it emphasizes the meaning.

Go down in pitch on anything you want to emphasize —on adjectives and verbs, words before commas, the ends of phrases, and, this may surprise you, the ends of questions. Drop your pitch at the ends of sentences too.

"People must be taught to make their voices fall at the ends of sentences," advises *The Art of Speaking,* and "to deliver a talk without any particular whine, cant or drawl, but with the natural inflections of voice which they use in speaking."

Don't make the mistake of underlining a word or phrase in your notes you want to emphasize. This will make you jump on the word in an unnatural way. Talk your talk out loud. Does it sound the way you'd say it sitting across the dining table from someone? Going down in pitch gives you the sound of authority.

Speaking too quickly, like Robert Kennedy, at the same pace all the time doesn't plant your thoughts. Everything sounds the same. Remember, 170 words per minute is a good pace. Give your listener time to let your message sink in. Use pauses; they are vocal underliners that say, "Think about it." Pause at the end of an important point, after an exhortation, a declaration or a question. Pause, eyes up, and your listener reflects.

Watch out for "y' know" and "uhhs" and "uhhhhms." New York City's Mayor Koch is the king of uh, uh, uh. He gets away with it somehow, but it makes others sound groping, unsure, nervous. If you have any of these speech tics, put a little red sticker with *uh* or *y'know* crossed out on your watch and it will get rid of the habit in two days.

Last of all, speak with momentum and energy. The walls of the room should give you back your own voice as you talk. That tells you you have the energy you need to infect the other person. You don't project by being loud, you project with energy. Quite different.

REMEMBER

Rehearse four times aloud as though in the real-life situation, seeing the most skeptical faces in front of you—Last rehearsal as close to delivery time as possible.

Speak with momentum.

Use the dining-table tone with energy behind it.

Keep your eyes up on openings, closings, declarations, ends of questions.

Eye sweep for the rhythm of listener attention.

3.
Antinervousness Control

What makes people nervous when they have to speak?

People are nervous because they're afraid of failure, of looking foolish and of not living up to expectations.

Try my -ATION process and never be nervous again.

It's Intelligent Anticipation that includes:
PreparATION
InformATION
EvaluATION
OrganizATION
FamiliarizATION

It's Physical Control through:
ExhalATION

It's Mental Control through:
Positive ExpectATION

The result is:
ApprobATION and AdmirATION

What are the specific steps to overcoming nervousness?

Once you've put your talk together and turned it into fast food for the eyes, and rehearsed in the most rewarding way, you've done 50 percent of the work toward preventing nervousness.

The other 50 percent of my foolproof method for eliminating nervousness is creating the look of authority; setting the scene for your talk; and the mental and physical control of nervousness: adjusting your attitude so that you go to the lectern with confidence, in control of yourself and your audience.

Will deep breathing relax you and prevent nervousness?

In spite of everything that's been written about the relaxing effect of deep breathing, big breaths make you tense. Take a deep breath. Feel your throat, feel how tense it makes the muscles in your neck. It's how you control the exhalation, not the inhalation.

The Sarnoff Squeeze

How do you prevent the shaking knees, dry mouth and butterflies?

I was in the theater for many years and until I was in *The King and I,* I went on stage every night with terrible stage fright. My heart would pound; I'd say to myself, Why am I here? But one night while I stood in the wings with Yul

Brynner, waiting to go on, I discovered the beginning of my physical control of nervousness. Yul Brynner stood there in the wings pushing a wall in a lunging position as though he'd like to knock it down, grunting as he did it. I said, "Yul, what do you do that for?" He said, "It helps me control my nervousness."

So I tried it, without the grunt, and sure enough, I never got stage fright again. Not only that, but the contraction of pushing the wall seemed to give me a whole new kind of physical energy. From then on, whenever I was waiting in the wings to do concerts, opera, nightclubs or television, I used this exercise of pushing a wall and— no nervousness.

When I became a public speaker, I couldn't very well go to the program chairman and say, "Excuse me, I feel a little shaky. I have to go push a wall." So I asked myself just what I was doing when I was pushing the wall. What could I do while I was waiting to go on that nobody would see and would give me the same control?

I discovered that what you do when you push a wall is contract the rectus abdominis muscles. These are the muscles that lie below the ribs where they begin to splay. This is the vital triangle. Contracting these muscles can have miraculous results.

To understand how these muscles work, try this. Sit down in a straight-backed chair. Carry your rib cage high, but not so high you're in a ramrod-straight military position. Incline slightly forward. Now put your hands together out in front of you, your elbows akimbo, your fingertips pointing upward, and push so that you feel an isometric opposing force in the heels of your palms and under your arms.

Say *sssssssss*, like a hiss. As you're exhaling the *s*, contract those muscles in the vital triangle as though you were rowing a boat against a current, pulling the oars back and up. Now the vital triangle should feel like you're tightening a corset. Relax the muscles at the end of your exhalation, then inhale gently.

Contracting those muscles prevents the production of noradrenaline or epinephrine, the fear-producing chemicals in your system. While you're waiting to go on, sit with your vital triangle contracting, your lips slightly parted, releasing your breath over your lower teeth on a silent *sssss*. You can do it anywhere without anyone noticing. And nothing, absolutely nothing will be able to make you nervous.

I've taught the Sarnoff Squeeze to thousands of people, often in strange places. When I showed it to former U.N. ambassador Jeane J. Kirkpatrick, we were in a restaurant having lunch. I've done it in ladies' rooms, taxi cabs and dinner parties.

The Sarnoff Squeeze is to nervousness what the Heimlich maneuver is to choking. Only the Heimlich maneuver is a remedy, and the Sarnoff Squeeze is a preventive. (By the way, if you ever do choke, do the Sarnoff Squeeze. It's the same as doing the Heimlich maneuver on yourself.)

While Joan Ganz Cooney was giving her commencement address at Smith College, she panicked for a second and then recaptured her poise by conjuring up a mental picture of me rowing a rowboat, pulling back the rectus abdominis muscles of the vital triangle. Her nervousness disappeared.

The Sarnoff Squeeze has other benefits. Besides preventing fear, it reduces any negative feelings like anger, depression, stress or fatigue, and generates energy.

I once had pneumonia while I was speaking in Hamburg, Germany. I had to fly to Toronto the next day to speak. I hadn't slept in nights. I was feeling very weak. But I revved myself up before I went on stage with the Sarnoff Squeeze and nobody ever knew there was anything wrong with me.

If you're under stress at the office, keep contracting that vital triangle on exhalation. It's like giving yourself a shot of adrenaline. I do the contracting all day long to energize myself.

This vital-triangle contraction also helps project the voice. The contraction gets the muscles under the diaphragm involved and helps send the air up out of the lungs with pressure to the vocal cords for projection. If your voice shakes from nervousness, the contraction will support your voice and prevent that quiver.

The Sarnoff Squeeze can control feelings of pain and cold. When you're queasy, it prevents nausea. If you're on an airplane and there's a lot of turbulence, use the Sarnoff Squeeze to counteract motion sickness.

If you're facing someone who intimidates you, the contraction will relieve your anxiety.

If you have a short fuse, the contraction will freeze-frame your anger and control it.

If you perspire profusely or have sweaty palms, the contraction will help.

Next time you're in the dentist's chair, contract. Next time you have to sink a twenty-foot putt, contract. Next time you ask your boss for a raise, contract.

The Sarnoff Squeeze acts like a brake; apply it every time you sense trouble ahead. Make it second nature, a reflex action—a tension, then a release of tension. That's how the squeeze works.

You'll use this physical control the rest of your life in what could be threatening situations and keep in control of yourself and the situation. Truthfully, it does more than any drug can do and it doesn't cost a penny. You'll find it may become addictive. I'm hooked on it. When you see what it does for you to prevent nervousness, you will be too.

Does this physical control work for everyone?

The treasurer of a large corporation stood at the lectern before an audience of his company's worldwide representatives and froze. I went up to the stage, put my arms around him and hugged him. "The most important thing Bob needs to know right now," I said to the audience, "is that we love him." The audience broke into enthusiastic applause.

"That's approval," I said. "Approval is what we all want on the lectern and are afraid we won't get. That's what makes us nervous. I'm going to give you all a free lesson in controlling nervousness."

I taught everyone in the audience the Sarnoff Squeeze. In five minutes I'd taken the pressure off Bob and given him a foolproof method for the physical control of nervousness. He began his talk again and this time delivered it with confidence and authority.

If you feel you're losing control of yourself and the audience, think Squeeze, and you'll get right back on track.

The Sarnoff Attitude Adjuster

How can you adjust your attitude for preventing nervousness?

71

Sports psychologists have discovered that attitude adjusting produces results for athletes preparing for competition. A member of the 1984 U.S. Olympic cycling team was very nervous going into the Olympics in Los Angeles. "My coach reminded me that I was a two-time national champion in that event, and Pan American champion at fifty kilometers. A lot of people in the race were going to be afraid of competing against me. He helped me adjust my attitude to focus on the thought that my competitors were fearful of me."

So the athlete put his negative feelings aside; he left wonder and doubt at the starting gate, and gave himself the competitive edge.

You never have to be a victim of the first attitude or behavior that comes to you. I was playing at the Drake Hotel in Chicago the Saturday night after John Kennedy was assassinated. I was so saddened, I didn't feel like performing at all—but the show had to go on. As I was singing, I noticed a little girl sitting with her parents at ringside. She looked so excited about being there that she captured my attention.

I was wearing a feather boa in a dream-sequence part of my act. When the number was finished, I went over to the child and wound the feather boa around her neck. She was so excited that I was infected by her excitement for the rest of my act. Her parents brought her up to my suite afterward to tell me it was her birthday, and I'd given her the best present she'd ever had. Actually, she gave me a present. Her attitude had changed my attitude.

What you say to yourself as you stand before your listener sends a message. If you tell yourself you're nervous, that's the message your listener receives.

Even a seasoned television newscaster like Diane

Sawyer attitude-adjusts before speaking in public. A keynote speaker at a New York luncheon honoring celebrated women of the 1980s, an observer reported, "Diane slipped out into the hall. I watched her standing all alone, psyching herself into readiness. By the time she faced the audience, she was relaxed, funny and very articulate. What struck me most was that she was in such control, so totally prepared."

So select the attitude you want to communicate the way you select an outfit from all the clothes hanging in your closet—by what is appropriate for the occasion. Attitude adjusting is your mental suit of armor against nervousness.

Let me add an aside how, as an actress, I used attitude adjusting. I was a singing actress but I was probably best known for the truth of my characterizations. I learned that if I concentrated deeply to communicate a feeling or a mood, I conveyed strong feelings to the audience.

My part of the humble head wife in *The King and I* was the shortest part I ever played on Broadway. Having so few lines, I didn't feel I could register strongly with the audience. So I devised for myself a technique to touch the audience in silence almost as much as I would if I were speaking.

As the cast took its place on stage, I'd stand in the corner and ask the other actors not to talk to me because I was going to work on motivating myself to communicate silent messages to the audience when the curtain went up. Since I played the part of a woman of great sadness and frustration, I murmured to myself, "My husband is dying, the king is dying. What will happen to the country? What will happen to my son? What will my world be like?" Then I took my position on stage, having frozen myself in the mode of maximum frustration and sadness.

When the curtain went up, the audience's attention focused on me through the intensity of my silent messages. Every night, when Mrs. Anna read her letter to the king, and got to these words—"utmost best"—I motivated the tears to tumble out of my eyes and down my cheeks. I got a Hollywood contract out of that performance. One producer came to see me cry sixteen times.

When I started my career as a public speaker, I thought I could use the same technique to motivate myself while I was waiting to go on. But it wasn't frustration or sadness I wanted to communicate. What message did I want to get across as a public speaker? I wanted to generate a warm feeling toward the audience that would prompt them to return the feeling and at the same time read me as a person of authority.

I chose to motivate three messages—joy, concern and authority. I hit upon four sentences that synthesize these messages. I call them motivating phrases. They give you confident thoughts before you go to the lectern and while you make a presentation. They send the vibes you want your listener to feel.

I'm glad I'm here.
I'm glad you're here.
I care about you.
I know that I know.

"I'm glad I'm here, I'm glad you're here," sends out the vibe of joy and ease, one of the five qualities of a good communicator. It expresses your pleasure in being there talking with them.

"I care about you," is the concern vibe. It says, I'm thinking about you. It energizes your face and eyes to show empathy for your listener.

"I know that I know," communicates the vibe of authority. If you've prepared well, you're entitled to say to yourself, I know that I know. It tells your listener you're in control. It gives you confidence and communicates the look of authority.

Say these four phrases several times quietly to yourself: I'm glad I'm here, I'm glad you're here, I care about you, I know that I know. Mumble the phrases under your breath. Vocalize the words or it doesn't get your brain working. Now try it again, faster. Think of it as a mantra, a psycher, a conditioner, a Hail Mary. It's a Hail Me, a Hail You.

Notice that the mantra starts out focusing on you—I'm glad I'm here. Then the attention switches to your listener—I'm glad you're here. It stays with your listener—I care about you; then the focus comes full circle back to you—I know that I know.

Think of the mantra as a circle. Imagine each phrase as the spoke of a wheel. As you say each phrase, the wheel turns. Now say the phrases again and make a circular motion in the air with your finger as you're saying them. Don't stop. You give a negative thought a chance to enter. Keep that wheel spinning round and round.

Come on, propel it around, the phrases chasing each other as fast as they can. Faster. It takes concentration to make the wheel run fast. Practice it until it's automatic.

This is the Sarnoff Mantra. You entertain only positive thoughts and expectation. You psych yourself, condition yourself. It has a stroking effect and soothes the body and the mind. You won't get nervous if you keep saying it over and over. It sends out positive vibes to your listener before you even open your mouth to speak.

I use the Sarnoff Mantra long before I'm in the auditorium waiting to go on. Months or weeks before, every time a group or audience I'm addressing comes to my mind, I say to myself, I love those people, I love that audience. I never let the Ooh-will-I-be-good-enough? thought get in. No matter who your audience is, if you go loving that group, they are never threatening to you.

Say the mantra to yourself while waiting to speak or present. The moment you leave your seat, you are in control of yourself and your listeners.

The Sarnoff Mantra propels you right up to the lectern. You won't be thinking negative thoughts. You'll be giving out those vibes—joy and ease, enthusiasm, sincerity and concern, and authority.

REMEMBER

Create a positive attitude
Say the Sarnoff Mantra—
      I'm glad I'm here.
      I'm glad you're here.
      I care about you.
      I know that I know.
Do the Sarnoff Squeeze—
      Contract the muscles of the vital triangle.

4.
Delivery:
Getting
and Holding
Attention

How do you capture audience attention immediately when you get up to speak?

Remember, your delivery begins at your seat before you go on. Your seat is the launch pad that shoots you up to the lectern. You're sitting on the launch pad, the engines in your rockets are fired up with the Sarnoff Squeeze, you're in control of yourself and your audience with the Sarnoff Mantra, it's all systems "GO."

You *stride* to the lectern, don't amble, *stride* with your eyes sweeping the room. You know your way there because you've rehearsed it. With your eyes up at the lectern, your peripheral vision lets you see where to put down your notes. You don't have to look down.

What makes good delivery?

Talk in the energized dining-table conversational tone, and speak with momentum—that's talking at a rate of about 170 words per minute. You infect your listener with your enthusiasm for your idea, product or service.

Remember, all openings must be totally eyes-up. You're 90 percent eyes-up the rest of the time. Glance down, pick up your next phrase from your notes, then eyes up and sweeping from wall to wall, the head moving right along with the eyes in one smooth, continuous movement. Your eyes communicate sincerity and concern.

Should you smile when you're speaking?

You want animation in your face . . . not smile, but love apples in your cheeks. You're saying to yourself I'm glad I'm here, I'm glad you're here . . . you communicate joy and ease. The message you're sending to your listener is Stop, look, listen . . . I'm in control here. That's the authority vibe.

What about gestures?

In *The Art of Speaking* we read, "The arms of the speaker are not to be heedlessly thrown out as if he were drowning in the pulpit or brandished after the manner of the ancient boxers exercising themselves by fighting with their shadow to prepare them for Olympic contests. Nor, on the contrary are his hands to be pocketed up, nor his arms to hang by his sides as lank as if they were both withered."

Stand at the lectern, your weight equally distributed on the balls of both feet, rib cage held high, both hands resting on the lectern. The left hand should be following your text. Your peripheral vision can inform you where your eye is due next. The other hand should be on the other side of your page, ready to slide it noiselessly aside when you've finished with it.

I don't teach hand gestures. I've never seen a good talk made better by gestures or a bad talk made good by hand gestures. If you use your hands well, use them. Hand gestures should anticipate and never follow your words.

The way you tell if your hand gestures work is to look at your listener's eyes. If his eyes are focused on your hands instead of your face, they're detracting from your message. Don't use them.

When you're not speaking at the lectern or making a presentation, hand gestures can take the place of words in communicating your message. The golfer Johnny Miller came to me before an important golf tournament for help in relating to the gallery. His fans were deserting him because he couldn't pay attention to the gallery and concentrate on his game at the same time. I suggested that while he walked from one hole to the other, he could wave to the gallery and smile. The crowd responded with applause and their support, and it didn't take anything away from his concentration.

Hand gestures can also defuse hostility. The former manager of a baseball team came to me because he had a problem with the fans. Every time he came out of the dugout, the crowd booed. He got mad; that made the fans angrier and they booed louder. I told him, when he went out on the field, to look up at the crowd in the stands, spread out his arms and smile. What does that gesture say to the fans? It says I'm yours. Do with me what you will. At that point, a crowd isn't going to go for blood.

Many political and religious leaders have used hand gestures as personal trademarks and a way of establishing a personal connection with their constituents. William Jennings Bryan, three times candidate for president, held his arms straight out at the sides and extended all the fingers as if to gather in the multitude.

Winston Churchill created the V for Victory gesture. Dwight Eisenhower carried the V-sign further, thrusting both arms into the air to make a V shape out of his entire body. John Kennedy perfected the three-finger wedge-shaped jab for emphasis, a gesture Gary Hart tried to appropriate for his 1984 presidential campaign.

Richard Nixon copied the Eisenhower arms-in-the-air gesture and added the Churchill V-sign with both hands, sometimes wiggling his fingers for emphasis. And the pope? With the arm raised, the palm facing downward, popes from Clemente VII to John Paul II have blessed the multitudes for centuries.

What do I do when something happens that I can't control?

I was right in the middle of giving a talk to the Four A's, the American Association of Advertising Agencies, in Boston when, over the loudspeaker system, a voice announced there would be a fire drill for the hotel staff. The voice kept droning on and on as I was speaking, more distracting to the audience than it was to me. To put them at ease, I told them a couple of stories.

"I'm used to this kind of interference," I said. "Years ago, I opened a nightclub act at the Hotel Fontainbleau in Miami, Florida, and Walter Winchell was there to review it. All of a sudden, Muzak came blaring out of the loudspeaker system and no one could shut it off. It played through my entire act. The orchestra played louder and I turned up my microphone, and I think I won.

"A far worse situation happened the night I was performing nine arias by Villa-Lobos at the Ziegfeld Theater. I played the part of a Colombian Indian princess. I wore a long braided wig and was barefoot.

"I was singing an aria down on my knees in front of John Raitt, who was the leading man, when a light drum exploded over my head and flaming slivers of glass fell on me. My wig caught fire but I just kept singing. John Raitt patted the flames on my head to put the fire out. We exited the stage to thunderous applause. The next day in the newspapers I was referred to as 'the singer with the singe on top.' "

So keep your cool and you keep your audience warm.

What's the best way to handle question-and-answer periods?

After you finish your talk or presentation, say, "Any questions?" If after two beats there's no response, say, "By the way, on the way in here, someone asked me . . ." or "I'm always asked . . ."

Don't have your listeners write down their questions and pass them to the speaker. It's dull. You lose the interplay between audience and speaker. Plant a few questions with colleagues in the audience to get things started. Hearing them usually gives other people in the audience the courage to participate with their own questions.

If someone asks you a question you can't answer, say so. And go on to the next one.

Distracting Behaviors

What behaviors are distracting?

Senator Patrick Moynihan was a speaker on the program with me at a conference in Bermuda. All through his talk, he was scratching his chest just below the collarbone. At the end of twenty minutes, there was a two-inch hole in his shirt. He also had the habit of saying uh, uh, uh, uh—searching for his word.

Later that day when we were talking in the lobby, I asked him if he'd like to get rid of the uhs and the scratching. He said he never could. I gave him a little red dot to put on his watch with the word *uh* written on it and crossed out. I said, "You look at your watch so many times a day. That red dot's going to remind you not to say uh." Also keeping both his hands on the lectern would prevent him from scratching. The next time he spoke he was uh-less and scratchless.

Many people who have nervous tics and have been seeing psychiatrists and psychologists for years to cure them have gotten rid of them with me in one or two hours.

The camera achieved in minutes what the couch in years hadn't.

When Deputy Secretary of State Warren Christopher was preparing for an interview program, he couldn't stop blinking as he talked. I told him he could only blink once at the end of each phrase. In five minutes of conversation, he totally redisciplined himself and blinked only at the ends of phrases.

An executive got involved in a sticky office situation. He was transferred to a rival team headed by a man he didn't like and couldn't work with. He developed a tic—it was a blink in one eye and a head jerk. The company suggested he see a psychiatrist. He asked if he could come to see me first.

I began by videotaping him in close-up from the chest up to the top of his head. All his tics were working. Then I put a book on his head and told him to stretch his head upward as hard as he could to keep the book steady there.

I videotaped him again in the same close-up shot, not showing the book. I played back both sequences. There he was on the second sequence, head still, eyes blinking normally. The tics disappeared.

One of the 1988 presidential hopefuls came to me with a habit of licking his lips every time he paused. Not one of his political aides had ever told him about it. I told him to close his mouth gently after every phrase so his tongue would not dart out in the pauses. That was the end of the habit.

What other behaviors distract listener attention?

At a board meeting, the woman executive opposite me sat for five hours pushing back the cuticles of her fingernails.

I was amazed that her cuticles weren't down to her second knuckle. No one had ever told her. Neither did I.

Costly nervous activities you want to watch out for are: twirling or playing with pens or pencils, drumming fingers on the desk or lectern, playing with paperclips. I role played with a CEO who kept bending and unbending paperclips all through our meeting. When I called his attention to it, he said, "My God, I've been nagging my fiancée to stop her nervous habit of saying 'ya' know,' 'ya' know,' 'ya' know.' But she never told me about this."

Doodling is one of the most costly nervous habits. It's an insult to the speaker. When he sees your pencil going round and round in the same place, he knows you're doodling. The speaker can interpret it as, I'm boring him, or, He's a nervous guy. But if the speaker sees your pencil moving across the page, he thinks, Now that guy's writing something important.

If you're a foot jiggler, control it by imagining you have a heavy ball and chain around your ankle. Restless fidgeting and moving around in your chair can rob you of presence. To control fidgeting, clasp your hands firmly together with tension and put them on the table or desk in front of you.

Hands in pockets is not always a no-no. Some women look jaunty with one hand in a skirt pocket; some men look appropriately casual. But watch out if the hands give the message they're uncomfortable and go into the pocket because they want someplace to hide. If you have coins in your pocket and jingle them, that makes us twice as uncomfortable.

Some mannerisms cheapen you. Millions of dollars are spent on the advertising of chewing gum. But it's better reserved for the privacy of your home. It may double your pleasure and double your fun, but it doesn't double the positive impression you give in public. The French don't put mirrors in their dining rooms because they consider the face looks its ugliest when chewing.

REMEMBER

Avoid:

Fidgeting

Twirling pencils, drumming fingers, playing
   with paperclips

Doodling

Knee jiggling or foot wagging

Hiding your hands in your pockets, jingling
   coins

Chewing gum

5.
Appearance: Everything About You Speaks

What is the importance of appearance when giving talks or making presentations?

How you look and what you wear is the packaging of the product—you. Corporations and professional organizations used to have dress codes, usually unspoken, rarely written down. It's against the law to impose dress standards or even talk to employees about dress or appearance, but everyone knows that how you dress is almost as important to your future in the firm as how well you do your job.

The CEO of a Fortune 500 company sent over one of his vice presidents, ostensibly to prepare for a talk he was going to give. He walked into the office wearing a green bow tie and a bright plaid sports coat, white socks and brown shoes. He looked as though he'd break into a buck-and-wing any minute. Boy, did he need help! His boss couldn't tell him what not to wear, but my camera could.

The camera and I can tell people a lot of things about their appearance that their bosses, aides or spouses can't or won't. William Casey, when he was director of the CIA, appeared for his first session with two huge bodyguards. The first thing I noticed was the dandruff all over the shoulders of his navy-blue suit. After we'd finished working on a talk he was preparing for his daughter's wedding, I said, "Mr. Casey, please don't be offended if I bring up something no one will tell you but me. I wonder if you realize that it looks as though it has snowed on your shoulders."

I said, "Before you leave the house in the morning, or before you go into a meeting, just glance down and quickly brush off the shoulders of your suit to make sure the distraction isn't there." He was very grateful for the suggestion. I also noted he had a wet handshake, so I showed him how to wipe his palm on the left side of his shirt under his jacket before he shook hands. It would just look as though he were adjusting his jacket.

What's the best way for women to dress when giving a talk?

"Neither in the tail nor vanguard of fashion be," said Shakespeare. You don't have to follow the latest fashion craze. Unfortunately, fashion today is more trash-ion than dashin'.

Watch your hemlines—others do. Bathing-suit-length hemlines will certainly get you attention but can be distracting on the job. Hemlines keep changing. Up down, up down! If you arrive at an interview with a hemline that is unfashionably long or short, you will look like a relic from another generation. Alexander Pope's advice, along with Shakespeare's, remains pertinent here: "Be not the first by whom the new are tried, nor yet the last to lay the old aside."

Too plain is an enemy. I say, have a look of *DASH*. I've been using that word ever since I've been in business. Ask yourself, How do my clothes make me feel? You should feel comfortable wearing them, and feel great about yourself when you wear them. If your clothes give you a lift, they'll give your talk or presentation a lift.

For women, the dress-for-success look is dead. The style was adopted to make women look equal. But we don't need that anymore. *New York Times* "Hers" columnist Nancy Bazelon Goldstone told how she went home for Thanksgiving and described to a male friend the suits, bow ties and briefcase she'd adopted for her job in the New York financial community. "Really?" he asked with interest. "What kind of aftershave do you use?"

Research done at New York University shows that women who choose this style are less secure or have less job experience than those who don't follow rigid rules. Women have or should have by now abandoned the uniform. They're turning now to an individual style. Colors are brighter, styles softer, European in cut. Dresses are in, as are suits that aren't a copy of menswear.

It's important for women over thirty to think about the neckline. The neck is the pedestal for your message giver, the face. Any neckline or collar that frames your face, or sets it off with a look of dash, is the most flattering look.

Don't have an unadorned neck. The large expanse of

unadorned neck captures the light and distracts your listener's attention away from your face.

Look for dresses or blouses that have higher necks. Add an interesting pin or a couple of chains. Sometimes a clunky necklace with large beads or stones will do the trick. Colorful scarves do wonders for a limited wardrobe and a limited budget. Hermes publishes a booklet that shows you how to wear scarves in more ways than you could ever imagine. Tie a scarf like a man's necktie, a robber's bandana, in a soft floppy bow, or wear it with one end folded over the other. Add a jeweled pin to the scarf or on the lapel of your suit.

Coming back from London on a plane, I admired the stewardess's necklace. She showed me that it wasn't a necklace, but a silk square scarf tied in a chain of knots the size of walnuts. She told me a friend had tied it for her and she'd left it that way because everyone admired it.

Avoid round peter pan collars or stiff man-tailored shirt collars. They look collegiate or little-girlish. A plunging neckline or an open shirt collar directs the listener's eyes downward and presents a wrong image.

Are some colors better to present in than others?

Helen Thomas, White House correspondent for United Press International, discovered during the Carter administration that when she wore a red dress to press conferences, the president called on her. The idea caught on. At the next press conference, twenty-seven women correspondents wore red.

One woman told me her boss asked her not to wear a bright color for presentations because she'd upstage her client. When you're presenting, why not be the center of attention? Have your color enter the room and claim attention with you. Wear a strong, rich color and it announces you with a fanfare.

Here are my thoughts on color:

> In red, you're ahead.
> Blue's for you.
> Green's in between.
> Brown is down.
> Black puts you in back.

Color also helps to give you a lift. Health columnist Jane Brody suggests that bright colors can banish the midwinter doldrums. "Red, yellow, orange, royal blue, kelly green, turquoise, hot pink are warm cheer-up colors," she says, "not just for you but for everyone who looks at you. The best lift of all is a brightly colored winter coat that you'll wear every day."

What about jewelry?

Necklaces that used to be called chokers are a plus. They cut the distance between your collarbone and chin, and help focus your listener's attention on your face. If you wear a high collar, long chains or ropes of beads or pearls are enriching.

Earrings give the face sparkle. Wear them with or without scarves at the neck. Avoid dangling ones. They have a life of their own. Their constant movement can be very distracting. They're okay for social situations and they're great for older women because they hide the tendons in the neck that become prominent with age.

Rings and bracelets can be a plus, but not too many rings and no noisy bracelets, please!

What about hair and makeup?

Well groomed is the first rule. Hair has to be in place and under control while you speak. Throwing your head back to get bangs out of your eyes and hair off your face is terribly distracting to the listener.

The mother of three very successful daughters told me that not one of them wears makeup. When she asked them why not, they said they felt so self-confident they didn't need it.

No matter how confident you feel or how successful you are, there are very few women whose appearance can't be improved by at least a touch of makeup. When you're standing at the lectern with butterflies in your stomach wondering what kind of an impression you're making on the audience, you want to know that you look the best you can look. A plain face with no makeup can look like a scared or uncertain face.

Giving a talk in a large auditorium doesn't mean you have to make up for a part in *Tosca*. But when lights are focused on you, you fade out and look pale. Under the lights, wear a little more makeup with a little more color. Lipstick is a must.

Makeup also gives the wearer a lift. Most women say they feel better in the morning after they put their makeup on. I don't think sculptor Louise Nevelson feels like Louise Nevelson until she puts on her eyelashes.

Remember to redo or refresh makeup just before you go on.

What should men consider in clothes?

The white shirt and inconspicuous tie used to be de rigueur for people in the financial field because it inspired trust. That's all changed. Executives today are dressing in blue suits, dark gray suits (but never brown suits), in pastel shirts and attractive complementary print ties. People in the creative professions have more leeway in their choice of clothes.

Nothing beats a dark navy suit for communicating the look of authority. When I advocated the navy suit, one of my clients said to me, "Everyone's in navy suits, so I wear a tan suit to look different." I said, "Do you look different and better or different and not as good?" The test is: Do you come across with authority? Gray suits may be as flattering as blue if you have a little gray in your hair.

Double-breasted jackets and jackets with side vents are out unless you're very thin. Secretary of State George Shultz was partial to double-breasted suits. I told him they looked fine when he was standing, but when he sat down they gave him a pouter pigeon look. He's much thinner now but he still looks better in the single-breasted suit and no vest.

Shirts should be blue or any pale pastel—pale peach,

yellow, pink. These are up colors. Why shouldn't men have the benefit and flattery of color in their clothes?

In my husband's office at Shearson-American Express they wait every day with great curiosity to see what color shirt he's wearing. He has a knack for putting together wonderful combinations based on his Turnbull & Asser shirts. He wears different shades of blue, pink, mauve, a few yellows. And his ties complement the color of the shirts. You look at him and you smile. His look makes you feel good.

White banker shirts are out. I was a guest lecturer at a financial conference when the audience got me involved in a big discussion about white shirts. One listener said, "If I go into a big meeting down south with Hiram Walker, what'll they think of me if I walk in there wearing a pastel shirt? They won't trust me." I said, "It's how you walk in there, how you present yourself, that makes your listener trust you, not a white shirt."

The chairman of a major car manufacturer came in wearing a drab tan shirt and a weary tan tie and brown shoes. I said casually, "Gee, if you're going to Las Vegas next week, you'd look great in a blue blazer and blue shirt." He very sheepishly turned over his necktie and opened his jacket to show me the numbers his wife had sewn into his clothes to coordinate his colors. But the numbers didn't match. He explained that his wife wasn't home that day and he'd attempted the color coordinating on his own—with disastrous results. He was color blind.

When he went home and told his wife about the blue suits and pastel shirts, she was so thrilled with the idea that they went right out and bought a whole new wardrobe.

Jane Brody suggests men wear shirts in pink or

salmon, brightly colored ties or ascots, a red wool scarf or red suspenders for a psychological lift.

The neck area is just as important for men as it is for women. I was asked to go to Israel to help Menachem Begin, the prime minister, prepare for Camp David. I'd observed his interviews here in the United States and I'd noticed that his shirts were white, and the collars were so loose that they made him look ill.

Before I went to Israel, I called Begin's staff to find out what size shirt he'd been wearing. I told his staff to buy a whole wardrobe of new shirts for him—one size smaller, in pastel colors, of course, with ties to complement them.

The first photograph taken of Begin after I'd worked with him was for the cover of *Time* magazine. I suggested he wear a blue suit and blue shirt for the picture. He said he'd have to ask his wife first. She gave her okay. So it was Begin in blue on the cover of *Time*.

The shirt collar should fit snugly around the neck and be cut in a style that covers your Adam's apple. An Adam's apple bobbing up and down can be very distracting to a listener. Tie your necktie firmly so that the knot is centered and close to your neck. A droopy necktie, like an open collar, draws the listener's attention downward away from your face. Avoid shirts with button-down collars. They look collegiate, unsophisticated; they tend to buckle around the neck and look sloppy.

Tie pins and collar pins to hold the collar in place look stiff. In Jimmy Carter's last days in the presidency he wore a tight collar clip that gave him a stuffy look.

Bow ties make people look lovable but not authoritative. They're great on Vladimir Horowitz—they go with his "pixie" look—but have too much of a look of naïveté for executives. Avoid bright colors or loud patterns. A print tie, preferably navy with a small figure or pattern, always looks right. The width of the tie should be about the same as the width of the lapel and the length of the shirt collar from neck to point, no matter what the current fashion. When lapels get wider, ties get wider and shirt collars get longer.

One very important note: Shirt cuffs should be showing about one inch below your jacket sleeve. It gives a touch of class.

For men, black is the best color for shoes. For some reason, brown shoes are distracting. They look wrong unless you're in sports clothes and wearing tan slacks.

When the newspaper columnist Bill Novack came to prepare for a television appearance, he was wearing a blue suit with brown shoes and socks that didn't cover his calves. Part of his bare leg showed when he was sitting down. Black shoes and longer socks gave him a finished look.

Speaking of socks. Peter Drucker, a popular economist, wore white socks when he gave a luncheon talk at the Waldorf Astoria. He sat on the dais swinging his leg with his white short socks falling down, exposing his bare ankles. It distracted terribly from what he was saying. Mens' socks should be long—up to the knee, and dark—never white.

At a recent conference with a group of oil executives, I pointed out someone in the audience I thought had really dressed for the part. He was wearing a navy suit, blue shirt, a printed tie. I asked him to stand up.

There were hoots and hollers all over the room. "You haven't seen his shoes," one of his colleagues shouted. He held up his foot and he was wearing, of all things, white shoes.

What about jewelry for men?

A man giving a slide presentation in one of my seminars wore a college ring on his middle finger that I found distracting. Another wore two rings on one hand. For men, wearing too many rings or wearing them on the wrong finger loses the look of authority.

What about hairstyles for men?

Men should avoid bangs. They hide the eyes, which is where you want to focus your listener's attention. Hodding Carter, Jimmy Carter's press secretary and now frequently seen on television, had what I call a scallop of hair over his forehead, dipping down almost to his eyebrows. I got him to comb his hair closer to his natural hairline so it didn't rob him of a third of his face. He instantly looked twice as strong.

Center parts are out: A man with a center part looks more like a choirboy than an executive. Changing to a side part gives you a look of greater presence.

A hairstyle can be too extreme. A handsome young advertising account executive had his hair cut like a marine sergeant's. It was almost punk looking. It didn't flatter him, but he liked it because it was the latest style. Six months later he called to tell me he'd abandoned it and people in his office were taking him more seriously.

What about beards and mustaches?

I love beards. They're so avuncular. We more instinctively trust men with beards (not straggly beards, though).

Cut and groom your beard as conscientiously as you do your hair.

"How a mustache dominates a face!" writes Otto Friedrich. "If Adolf Hitler had shaved his upper lip and then gone out for a walk, would anyone have recognized him? Or a freshly shaved Errol Flynn? Or Groucho Marx?"

Psychologists like to say that mustaches are "adornments of concealment." Although the wearer's intention is to adorn the body, his real purpose, they say, is to hide something he's insecure about. Columnist Russell Baker traces the rise in the popularity of the mustache to the increasing use of alcohol and drugs, which cause "young men to rise from their beds each morning too shaky to shave their kissable region without leaving ghastly scars."

Men wear mustaches for one of three reasons—to look older, to hide bad teeth, or because their wives like the way they tickle. Some mustaches improve the wearer's appearance, but many detract. If a mustache calls attention to itself, like the Fu Manchu mustache, it goes. Sometimes I feel like Delilah, I've had so many men shave off their mustaches.

To find out if your mustache is a plus or a minus, do the finger shield test. Go to the mirror, hold your index fingers over your mustache on each side, then talk. Do you look better with or without it? If you're not sure, get an objective opinion. (Your wife is not objective.) If you're more attractive without it, take it off.

No matter what time you present, it's important to be clean-shaven. If it means shaving twice in the same day, do it.

As long as we're talking about hair, let me tell you about the huge difference eyebrows can make in your appearance. One of our older senators asked me to counsel him with a video camera in the living room of his house in Washington. He shuffled into the room very slowly. He talked very slowly. He looked old.

At the right moment (you always have to make certain to choose the right psychological moment when you bring up a sensitive issue), I said, "Senator, you're doing three things that rob you of the look of energy in a man I know has energy: Number one: when you walk into a room, any room, stride; Number two: speak with momentum; Number three: is your wife upstairs? Does she have any mascara? Could she bring it down?"

The senator had beautiful white hair, but also white eyebrows, which caught the television spotlight and said "old." I used brown mascara on his eyebrows to show him that if he dyed his eyebrows brown, he would look fifteen years younger. I haven't seem him with white eyebrows since.

For Texas congressman and Speaker of the House Jim Wright, bushy, overgrown eyebrows are his personal trademark. They've been favorably compared to the tail fins of a 1961 Buick. In trying to slick him up for television, even the most persuasive media consultants were reluctant to suggest he cut them. "Without substance, image is empty," contends Wright. So the eyebrows stay.

Men and Women

What do you wear if you're giving a talk at a resort?

If your speaking engagement or presentation takes place in an informal setting, you might think a jacket and tie aren't appropriate. But instead of dressing like your audience, dress for authority. Even if your audience is dressed in golf shirts and sports slacks, wear a tie, shirt and sports jacket. Turtlenecks make you look too casual.

Dressing more formally than your listener almost always works in your favor, no matter what the situation. An image consultant was hired by an accounting firm in Los Angeles to polish its image. The firm's president was convinced that celebrities wearing gold chains and leather wouldn't give their business to accountants wearing suits. The consultant persuaded the firm's employees to stick with their suits and the firm now has nineteen offices.

The same advice goes for women, too. You enhance your authority in any presentation situation by dressing up rather than down. Never wear pants for presentations. If you're speaking on an evening program and you know your audience is coming straight from work, wear something you'd wear to the office when you knew you were going out to the theater afterward. On the other hand, don't overdress.

Do heavy people have more trouble communicating authority?

It takes longer to trust or be persuaded by people who are overweight. The impression is that if you don't have the discipline and judgment to do what's right for you, you won't have the discipline to do what's right for your company.

In a recent corporate seminar in Houston, a top executive was five-foot-ten and weighed 205 pounds. He confided he had a hard time being taken seriously in the company because of his weight. I asked him when his birthday was. It turned out to be just three days before mine. I said, "Give both of us a birthday present. Lose thirty pounds." He did.

I made a deal like that with a bright young advertising trainee. I showed her a close-up of herself on the video playback. She was stunning—violet Liz Taylor eyes and dark brunette hair. Then I pulled back the camera and she saw she was twenty-five pounds overweight. I told her I'd give her a free session if she lost twenty pounds. Six months later she came back—thirty pounds lighter. The incentive was seeing herself on videotape in close-up—as a beautiful young woman.

Is it better to appear without glasses?

Not only do glasses glare, but they rob you of two important message givers, your eyes and your face. There's a slight veil between your eyes and their eyes.

Glasses with metal frames and a double bar across the nose are the worst offenders. They are unflattering and a distraction.

Menachem Begin's black licorice eyeglasses made him look sinister. I called ahead to Israel to tell him to get new frames before I came to work with him. He did, right away.

If you can't see your audience without your glasses, you have three choices. You can deliver your opening remarks without your glasses, then slip them on for the rest of your talk. You can wear glasses with nonglare lenses that do not reflect the light and let your eyes show through. In fact, they look as though there are no lenses in the frames at all. Or you can get contact lenses.

Most of my clients discover it isn't as hard as they think it is to present without their glasses. If you've printed your talk in large black letters, you'll be able to talk from it without your glasses. If you've numbered your phrases on the left and follow them along with your finger, you won't lose your place. If you've rehearsed your talk at least four times out loud so that you're familiar with it, you'll know it well enough not to have to read it.

Nobody can see to the back of a large auditorium or conference hall, even with 20/20 vision. If you look as though you intend to make eye contact with your listener, he'll take the intention for the deed.

REMEMBER

Color
Neck area
Style
Jewelry
Hair
Beards and mustaches
Makeup
Glasses

6.
Ambiance:
Room Setups
Make a Difference

What do you need to know about the room you'll be speaking in?

How large is the room?
How is it arranged?
Is there a speaker's lectern and a microphone?
Is the lectern on a stage or level with the audience?

Find out from the program coordinator in advance, and you can set the scene of your talk to suit you. You will know ahead of time the environment you'll be speaking in and this will prevent any last-minute surprises that could upset you.

When you stand at a lectern in front of an audience, the lectern becomes your pedestal. It gives you presence and authority. The lectern has to be high enough so you don't hunch over it to see your notes, and low enough so that you don't stand on tiptoe to pick up your next phrase.

Samuel Newhouse, who built the new Samuel I. Newhouse School of Communication at Syracuse University, was five feet tall. When he gave the address formally opening the school, he stood at the lectern wearing a mortarboard. All the audience saw from where they were sitting was a mortarboard bobbing up and down. If you're short, you'll need at least a three-inch riser to stand on.

If you're tall, you'll need the lectern shelf raised. Fortunately, most lecterns today are adjustable. If not, use a telephone book to raise your notes to a comfortable level.

Check to make sure the shelf of the lectern is inclined. You want to have your notes as high as possible on the lectern so that your eyes have the shortest distance to travel between your notes and the listener's eyes.

You need a ledge on the shelf to keep your notes from sliding off onto the floor.

When a ledge is too low, make one at the right height for yourself. Place a ruler where you want your ledge to be. Use Mortite, or window putty, to hold the ruler down. (In a pinch, you can use chewing gum.)

It's a good idea always to take along a sheet of white paper and transparent tape to cover the podium lamp so that it softens the light hitting your face and doesn't spotlight your Adam's apple.

What's the best chair setup for the room?

When I gave my first seminar years ago in the Hotel St. Moritz on West 59th Street in New York, the hotel furnished Louis XVI–style chairs with deep, broad, upholstered seats and straight backs. I've used this kind of chair in my seminars ever since.

The seats are large enough and the backs tall enough with solid back support for almost everyone to sit in comfortably—even a basketball player, and I've had more than one as a client. A straight sit-up chair is the ideal chair for listening. When your listener is more erect, he 's more attentive.

How the chairs are arranged is very important for listener response. You want the first row as close to you as possible. A chasm between speaker and audience keeps you from connecting warmly with your listeners.

Chairs in straight rows, or long rows of chairs without a center aisle, make the room feel cold, anonymous. Talking to the American Association of Advertising Agencies in Boston, I was scheduled to follow Ken Blanchard, the author, after the coffee break.

While everyone was taking a break, I went into the auditorium and saw that the chairs were arranged straight across. The room had all the conviviality of a movie theater. During the break, a busboy and I rearranged the chairs in a semicircle with an aisle down the center.

So send a diagram ahead to the program chairman of how you like the room set up, in an arc or a semicircle, with a center aisle. This arrangement makes for a friendlier room. Your listeners see each other's reactions, and respond to each other as well as to you. It creates a warmer, more intimate atmosphere even in a huge auditorium.

If I'm making a presentation in an office, what should I do about the room setup?

In an office meeting, an oval or round table is the best shape for communicating your message. It breaks down bureaucratic hierarchies and power relationships, and gives you equal access to everyone.

Most offices, though, have rectangular tables. So position yourself at the head of the table, and ask your listeners to pull out their chairs a little bit and angle them slightly to face you. This gives you easy access to the listeners' eyes.

In a one-on-one situation in an office, pull up your chair close to the desk and imagine you're talking across a dinner table. If the client comes to you, sit behind your desk. It gives you more authority, but pull up a comfortable armchair across from the desk for him. He feels more comfortable and more important.

Armchairs make you equals; armless chairs demote you. If you want someone to feel inferior, give him a chair without arms. I always put a pompous person in an armless chair—it's a psychological downer.

How important is lighting?

Not so long ago, I was scheduled to give a talk to twenty-four hundred people at the Sheraton Hotel in New York. I went down there a few days before to look over the room. There was a luncheon going on at the time. The room was almost in total darkness. The speaker's face was lit on only one side. One-sided lighting makes speakers look sinister. I spoke to the banquet manager and arranged with him to have full-front lighting for my talk.

Full-front lighting on your face is the most flattering at the lectern. At the dress rehearsal of *The King and I*, Gertrude Lawrence taught me a lesson in lighting. With a pocket mirror, she paced the entire stage to check that the lighting fell where it should on her face and that the color of the light was the flesh-pink tone that flattered her.

A woman should check the light with a pocket mirror before she goes on. (A man doesn't have a mirror handy so he'll have to ask someone.) See that it lights your whole face and that your eyes are not dark pockets. Full-front lighting flatters the face and illuminates the eyes. You can't reach your listener's heart and soul without eye contact. Eyes in shadow are blank eyes, eyes with no message to give.

Woman hath no greater enemy in any communicating situation than fluorescent light. It's harsh and unflattering. Many top cosmetic firms are my clients. I've been begging them to develop a makeup for women to counteract the ugliness of fluorescent lighting in most offices. No results yet.

Think of how different you feel under incandescent lighting and under fluorescents. Incandescent light is flesh pink—it's warm. Fluorescent is blue—it's cold. Fluorescent light doesn't show anybody at his best. Scientists have discovered that rats become more restless and nervous when exposed for long periods to fluorescent light. Do you realize the effect it has on you while speaking or making a presentation?

So always check out the room; find out about the light. If your speaking engagement is in a distant city, send your requirements ahead. When you arrive at your speaking engagement, go to the auditorium at least an hour or two before you go on. It's never too early and you should never be too busy to devote the time you need to give yourself the best chance of presenting in a favorable setting.

How do you check out the sound system?

Listening to a speaker you can't hear is like watching television with the sound turned off. The listener concentrates on other things instead—like the way you move your mouth.

Check the sound system of the room before you give your talk. Get the sound technician to listen while you stand at the podium and speak into the microphone. Is the sound level appropriate? Ask for more bass in the sound than treble. This gives you a lower, richer sound.

Get a feeling for the distance between you and the microphone. Don't lean into the mike. If you're using a handheld microphone, hold it at mouth level, but not too close to your mouth or you'll pop your p's. People using hand mikes tend to pace up and down like a lion in its cage. You have more of a look of authority if you stand still.

When you're speaking in a small room or to a small group of people, ask yourself if you really need a mike. If you project your voice with energy—not volume—and the walls give you back your voice as you speak, you don't need amplification.

What's the ideal room temperature for listener attention?

A room that's too warm dulls a listener, especially if you're talking after lunch. Air conditioning that raises goosebumps on your listener's arms turns his thoughts away from you, to escape. Smoky or stale air also makes a listener restless. It cuts off the oxygen supply to the blood and makes breathing more strenuous.

A slightly cool temperature in a room with freely circulating air gives you the best environment for holding your listener's attention. Sometimes you can't do anything about these conditions. But ask.

Is there anything else I should do before I deliver my talk?

The last thing to do in setting up the room is to make a dry run—walk from your seat up to the lectern. Watch out for wrinkles in the carpet or electric wires that could trip you up. If your feet are familiar with the terrain, your eyes can be up all the way from your chair to your attention-grabbing opening.

REMEMBER

> Room
> Lectern
> Chairs
> Lighting
> Sound
> Temperature

How do I know if I'm a commanding speaker?

It's time to get out the videotape equipment again. This is your After Picture. Get someone to work the camera. Stand with body tension for attention in the same place you stood for your Before Picture, wear clothes that give you the look of authority, deliver your talk as though in the real-life situation, eyes up and eye sweeping, contracting the vital triangle, spinning the Sarnoff Mantra.

Before you play back the After Picture to see how you did, look at your Before Picture. Now play back your After Picture. You'll see immediately how far you've come.

Where do you see the difference? Mostly around the eyes.

Before: The eyes have a negative expression.

After: The eyes are assertive. The tension in those muscles caused by wonder and doubt are gone.

Before: You look unsure of yourself at the lectern.

After: You have presence, authority.

Before: You look stuffy and uptight.

After: Without glasses, your face radiates joy and ease. The expression on your face is animated.

Before: Your delivery was flat, constrained.

After: You have energy, momentum. You are 100 percent freer than before.

The After Picture—confident and nervousness free—is you.

ACES For Ad Libs and Introductions

How do you deal with giving an ad-lib talk?

Go to conferences or meetings anticipating that you'll participate. Even if you're attending a conference and you haven't been scheduled to speak, there's a good chance you'll be asked to contribute anyway. What do you have to lose by preparing something ahead of time?

If you get caught at the last minute and have to come up with something from scratch, here's a guide to help you. Think of it as the Four Aces for Ad-libbing:

A: Attention Getter
    Allusion to Audience Interest
    Anecdote, Analogy
    Advice
C: Commitment
    Course of Action
    Concern, Cure
    Charge, Challenge

E: Evidence
   Example
   Experts' Opinions and Quotes
S: Socko Conclusion
   Suggestions
   Solutions
   Sense of Direction
   Send to Action

Jot down two or three ideas while others are talking, put the ideas into a logical sequence, think of an opening that's unpredictable and a closing that has clout, and you've got yourself a talk.

A friend of mine always has a stock of quotes in his head and can produce something appropriate at the drop of a hat. Collect your own for occasions like these. Never leave a meeting without leaving behind some thought or idea on the table.

What if my boss or colleague gets sick at the last minute and asks me to step in for him and make a presentation?

Open with the light touch. Say something like, "Aren't you glad I'm here? The whole thing could have gone down the drain without me." Or, "Some understudies go on to make brilliant careers when the headliner doesn't show."

Use his talk and his slides. If you make a mistake, kid around. Say, "That's what I get for using someone else's material." A star is born.

How do you get the person who introduces you to give you the right introduction?

Other people's introductions rarely do anything to heighten the listener's interest in you. After years of being introduced by misinformed, unexciting and overly complimentary speakers, I now write my own introductions and send them ahead. The introducers are grateful.

What about introducing speakers?

On a dinner program featuring the adventurer and mountain climber Sir Edmund Hillary, eight people sat on the speakers' dais along with him. Before Hillary spoke, every single one of those eight people got up to recount his experience with Hillary. Not one of their introductions was under ten minutes long. You could see Hillary getting madder and madder.

Then the chairman got up to introduce Hillary and took another ten minutes. That made a total of not less than one hour of introductions.

Hillary finally went to the lectern, spoke for three minutes about his raft trip down the Colorado River, and sat down. Can you blame him?

Introductions—and that means total introduction time —should never be longer than one minute. That's 170 words on the page. Unless it's for a returning hero. And those are rare.

Visuals:
The Best Way
to Use Them

*What do I have to check out for presenting with slides
or other visual aids?*

David Ogilvy once said that the demons of presentations
are visual aids. They have the greatest potential for going
wrong.

You can never check enough to see that your slides
are loaded correctly, that the machine you're using func-
tions healthily. Many of them get sick while performing.
Many a CEO is embarrassed by slides jamming in the
projector. Down the drain goes his presentation.

You've heard of Murphy's Law and Parkinson's Law.
Well, here's Sarnoff's Law: the risk of disaster with visual
aids is in direct proportion to the technical complexity of
your equipment situation. For an important talk or presentation, arrange to have a technician standing by at all
times—for a rehearsal and during your presentation.

When you send your requirements ahead, let them

know what kind of visual aids you'll be using. Be as specific as you can. See that your slide carousel is compatible with their slide projector. However, you're much safer if you take your own carousel already loaded—triple checked. Tell them if you're using half-inch or three-quarter-inch videocassettes so that they have the appropriate equipment.

When you arrive, make sure everything you asked for is there too. Position the equipment where you want it. If you're using an overhead projector, ask for a table that has plenty of room on the right and left sides of the projector. Have the projector stand or table on your right and about an arm's length from where you're speaking. Position your easel for a flip chart or storyboard presentation where the audience can see it easily.

When you get the visual aid located where you want it, mark its position with a piece of masking tape in case it gets moved. Now turn on the projector. Check the focus and the framing. Use cassette cases, books, whatever's handy to raise the projector. It's a good idea to tape a large piece of cardboard to the projector to screen the light so it doesn't glare in the audience's eyes.

Bring your slides or acetates or video cassettes when you're checking the equipment. Try to have someone else work the slide projector for you so that you can avoid fumbling with the controls. If you must operate the equipment yourself, familiarize yourself with it well in advance.

If you're changing your own slides, tape the hand control to the lectern so it stays in place while you're talking.

Have a spare projector bulb on hand for a sudden blowout. You'll want to set up some kind of system for turning on and off the lights—say, a verbal cue for the electrician.

What do you have to know for presenting with slides or other visual aids?

As one executive said in a talk called "The Care and Feeding of the Executive Speaker," "You've heard the proverb, one picture is worth a thousand words?" He continued, "If you believe that, draw me the Gettysburg Address."

A woman dressing for a party sits in front of the mirror. Her hair is beautifully done, her dress elegant. Now she's ready to put on the finishing touch. She takes out her jewelry box. Before she selects her jewelry, the question she should ask about each piece is, Do I need it?

The next time you use visual aids, in deciding whether to use each one, ask yourself: Do I need it? Nine times out of ten, the answer is no.

Depending on visual aids to get your message across sends a signal right off the bat to the audience—either your written material or your personal chemistry or both aren't up to the job. These are the message givers that communicate your message, not pictures.

Most people say they use visuals to underline a point. You don't need visuals for that. Emphasize your points with your voice and forget the slides. But sometimes when presenting statistical material, you will need visual aids.

What's the best way to prepare visual aids?

For that one time out of ten that you have to use visuals, follow these general rules:

1. The visual should be interesting and imaginatively designed. So many corporate people use tenth-rate slides. Good visuals are clear, colorful and aesthetically pleasing. Bright, interesting visuals catch your listener's attention and help him retain your message. Don't overload your visual with information. Keep writing to a minimum. Never use ordinary typewriter lettering. It's hard to read and boring.

   When possible, use pictures or designs instead of words. For example, if you're talking about your increasing share of the fresh-milk market, use graduated-size milk bottles to show growth instead of a rising line. Keep images simple and large—about two inches high for every twenty feet between the screen and the audience.

   A strip of bright color across the top or down the side does wonders to energize dull columns of numbers. Code your information or statistics by color or shape if possible so you can refer to the visual without pointing to it. Use colored grease pencils to brighten up acetate visuals.

2. Your words should be legible thirty-two feet away.

3. Know the life span of your visual. Does your listener finish with it before you do? If so, it's on the screen too long. But don't hurry it. Pull your visual too soon, and the listener feels cheated.

4. Never say in your talk what's written on the visual. Your audience can read. You're up

there to give the big picture. Let your visuals give some of the details.

5. Use anecdotes or examples to vary the pace of your visual presentation and to add verbal color to the visuals.

   The best presenter with visuals is David Ogilvy, who is a master of any kind of talk or presentation. He spices up his visual presentations with interesting, appropriate short anecdotes from his experience.

6. Always talk over the change of slide or overhead so you don't lose momentum in your delivery. A long silent pause while you wait to see if the right slide appears on the screen loses listener attention and your own train of thought.

7. Never leave the screen blank. A lighted screen is a distraction. Put in a black slide.

8. Don't present visuals in a pitch-dark room. It makes people sleepy. Turn the lights halfway up.

Here are eleven rules from a speech by David Ogilvy. We disagree a bit on number 5.

1. Always *rehearse*. Get your timing right, and shoot anyone who runs over. "Give him the hook" as they said in vaudeville.

2. Always have a super-terrific operator for your projectors. A projectionist can make or break a presentation.

3. Keep the temperature of the room at 71 de-

grees. Any warmer, and your audience will go to sleep. Any colder, and they feel miserable.

4. Never have any empty seats. Always have a full house—even if it means meeting in the lavatory.

5. When you show slides, always make them legible, and always read out *exactly* what is printed on the slide. Nine out of ten presenters put up a slide and talk about something else. There is no surer way of losing your audience.

6. Beware of *vampire electronics*. They steal the show away from what you are trying to sell. I shall never forget the brilliant film that Charles Eames made for IBM at the World's Fair in New York a few years ago. Nobody who saw it could understand what it was trying to say. Same thing with the show put on by the Czechs at the Montreal World's Fair; everybody knew it was brilliant—it had to be, with thirty projectors. But nobody got the message.

7. Only use your *best* speakers. If your boss is a lousy speaker, keep him off the program—or get another boss.

8. Don't have your convention in Las Vegas. Have it in London! When twelve thousand American lawyers came to London for the American Bar Association convention a few years ago, they started something. Today, more international conventions are held in London than anywhere else in the world.

9. If you want audience participation, don't run risks. *Plant* your interruptions and your questions with reliable friends in the audience.

10. Never have meetings on Sundays. It is anti-Christian.
11. Always hold a post-mortem. This way, you won't repeat the same mistakes the next time. Poll everyone who came to your meeting and find out what bored them most.

When I was a speaker at a large convention in Mexico, I went to hear one of the other speakers, a well-known executive headhunter, talk to an audience of three thousand people. He presented his talk in his shirtsleeves, pacing back and forth on the stage, groping for words and trying to unscramble his visual aids.

The woman sitting next to me moaned and groaned all the way through his talk. "What's the trouble?" I asked her. She said, "That's my husband up there." Her husband subsequently became a client, and now is one of the most wonderful speakers you can hear—with or without visuals.

Never start a visual presentation with visuals. Take two or three minutes to establish yourself and presence. This gives you authority.

Presentations with visuals have to be choreographed. You must coordinate changing the visuals as you speak, orchestrate movements and words.

Change your visuals smoothly. Glance quickly to see that the right visual is on the screen, then turn full face to the audience, eyes up and eye sweeping, and talk. You want to be in profile to the audience as little as possible. Have a photocopy of your visual aids on the podium so you'll know what's on the screen without having to look at it constantly.

Refer to what's on the slide by pointing to it verbally: "You'll see the increase in sales on the yellow panel," or

"The red oval shows market expansion." Don't use pointers. They make you look like a teacher.

If you do have to point at your visual, refer to it with your extended arm and finger. Keep pointing and turn to the audience, talking. Remember: Touch, turn, tell. You want to be 90 percent eye to eye with your audience.

What advice do you have for presenting with an overhead projector?

Acetates used on the overhead projector are inclined to look cheap if they're nothing more than typewritten pages. They're boring. Use imagination in creating acetates. Try color grease pencils to make them bright and lively.

Some of our more sophisticated corporations have come in with very exciting acetates using black backgrounds with bright red print, or multicolored backgrounds with black printing. This costs more and takes time to prepare, but the effect is well worth it.

You may not have the time to prepare fancy acetates, and your company may not want to spend the money. But I urge you at least to use grease pencils to put in some color. You can't imagine what a difference it makes. Hand printing in color looks very dynamic.

If you design an acetate with sequential points, use a piece of paper to mask the information you want to conceal. Move it down point by point to reveal your information.

To get your acetate slides straight on the projector your first try, make a slide guide for the projector. Cut a strip of cardboard about an inch wide. Attach it with masking tape to the upper edge of the projector to act as a straight edge for the acetate. Place your acetate right up against this guide and it will always be straight.

What about the choreography of presenting with the overhead projector? I call it the triangle tango. Stand beside the projector table. The table should be at least two feet deep to accommodate three zones: the projector, the feeding zone, and the discard zone. It works like this: The feed zone of the acetate slides forms the A corner of the triangle, the projector the B corner of the triangle, and the discard zone is the C corner.

Place the pile of acetates to feed close to you at the back of the table. Feed the new acetate to the projector with your right hand, and discard the acetate on the projector with the left hand at the same time.

The pile of acetates should be the same height as the projector surface—use a book to raise them to the same level. This eliminates up and down movement that's distracting to the audience. Work clockwise from A to B to C and back to A again. If you're left-handed, reverse the order.

The triangle tango eliminates nervousness by preventing you from missing an acetate, repeating an acetate, placing the acetate on the projector upside down. It saves motions that cost you momentum. It looks smooth and professional.

What's the best advice for 35mm slide presentations?

Clients have come with fifty slides for a thirty-minute presentation. Just because those slots in the slide carousel are there, don't think you have to fill every single one. Remember, when presenting with slides: less is more.

121

Color, color, color—make the slides as colorful as possible. Use pie charts, designs or pictures instead of words wherever you can.

You can never check your carousel enough to see that everything is in sequence and right side up. Of eight possible ways to insert a slide in a magazine carousel, only one will project your slide correctly.

Mark slides with a number in the upper right corner to make sequence checking easy. Your slide numbers should match the carousel numbers and the numbers in your script.

Even if you've loaded the carousel, fitted the security ring and taped it yourself at home, check the slides and monitor the focus once more when you get to the auditorium or conference room. Do this by projecting the slides on a sheet of white paper you hold about three feet away from the projector lens. Adjust the focus and check your slides.

The projector should be already running before you begin your presentation. This isn't a distraction if you've loaded your carousel with black slides first and last. Talk over your slide changes; don't stop to wait for the change. Your slide must always arrive a split second before your words do. As with overheads, know the life span of your slide and don't let it die there on the screen.

Have the room semi-darkened so you can see audience reaction. You'll know whether to move faster or slower.

What's the best way to use flip charts?

I've rarely seen anyone get the page flipped over on the first try. Also, they make a crunching sound that's distracting. They're not for auditorium presentations, but they're okay for meetings with small groups and for brainstorming sessions.

Flip-chart pads with standard white paper are preferable to newsprint-quality paper, which bleeds when you use fresh felt-tip markers. Print your message, don't use script. The letters should be no less than four inches high so they're legible from the back of the room.

If you write on charts as you talk, your back is to the listener. To facilitate the whole procedure, pencil in lightly the words you'll be writing, then go over them in marker when you make your presentation. Keep talking while you're writing.

Position the easel so that everyone can see it. Make sure the shelf holding your pad is high enough so that the whole chart is visible.

The choreography for a flip chart is the same as it is for the overhead and slide presentation—touch, turn and tell. There's always that little bit of suspense—will you get the page over the top of the easel or won't you? Dog-ear each page for quicker flipping. Rehearse your page turning ahead of time so you can do it in one smooth, continuous movement.

What about presenting with storyboards?

Board presentations are great for advertising campaigns, architectural layouts or interior design plans. Small boards look cheap and don't make much of an impression on your listener. Big boards get your message across.

The golden rule of board presentations is: you're in the concealment business until you want to introduce a new feature. Stack your entire set of boards on the easel to begin with. Make sure the ledge on your easel is wide enough to accommodate them all. Then take away each card as you talk. This makes for a much smoother presentation than placing cards on the easel as you talk. Pile your used cards on a chair or table nearby.

Remember, give a split second's attention to the board, then turn your attention to the audience, eyes up and eye sweeping.

REMEMBER

Less is more
Imaginative design
Color, color, color
Timing
Touch, turn, tell

Facing the Camera and Keeping Cool in the Hot Seat

How should I prepare to appear on television?

The chances are a hundred to one you'll be facing a video camera in the next few years in your business or professional life. You may be facing television interviewers, presenting your idea, product or service on video cassette, or participating with your colleagues in a teleconference.

Only a few years ago, the policy of large corporations like Texaco was to avoid the media. "Our theory was," said Kerryn King, senior vice president, "it's the spouting whale that gets the harpoon. If a TV reporter called, asking for an interview, we just said no. . . . Now we reach out to reporters. We hold press conferences and open houses."

The reason for the change in policy? It's worth about a million dollars in free advertising. Michael Barratt, an English speech consultant, says, "A company might have to spend two hundred thousand dollars to get a minute's exposure on television. Just think how valuable an invitation to a member of your staff to do a three-minute-to-an-hour interview could be. They're effectively offering you a blank check and asking you to come and cash it."

The media is hungry for programming in the area of finance. Look at the popularity of programs like "Adam Smith's Money World" and "Wall Street Week" on public television, and the success of financial programs on cable.

How are corporations reacting to the public demand for news of takeovers, stock-market tips and economic forecasts? By training their executives to present themselves in the media with presence and authority. "Without this sort of training," says Derek Dewey-Leader, the senior press official of a British corporation, "industry is letting its executives be led like lambs to a slaughter."

It's appalling when the CEO of a Fortune 500 company appears on network television or on an influential financial program, as one did recently, and does not come across as a strong leader. He was weak on content, on ideas and on how to deliver his message. He seemed to be groping. He couldn't answer the interviewer's questions and he ahhed and uhhmed his way through the interview.

His appearance didn't help either. He wore a light suit, tinted glasses, striped shirt, striped tie, and socks that were too short to cover his calves. He certainly did not enhance the image of his company.

Any business or political leader who wants to make his media appearance profitable for his idea, product or service has to impress the audience with credibility and infect them with passion.

I was recently invited to England by one of the London television stations to evaluate the media appearances of Margaret Thatcher and some of England's top political leaders. One of England's most persuasive and dynamic speakers on television is Labour Party leader Neil Kinnock. He often moves the audience with his energy and enthusiasm, even people who don't support his politics.

About twenty of my clients appear on television somewhere in the country each week. In addition to corporate executives, I prepare authors, newscasters, talk show hosts, and political candidates—from state assembly members right up to presidential hopefuls—for media appearances.

A woman who is now an outstanding newscaster came to me several years ago. She was then working as a reporter at one of the network affiliates. She wanted to be an anchorperson but couldn't get the job.

She walked in wearing heavy tortoiseshell glasses; she had no animation in her face; she wore clothes that didn't do anything for her. When she spoke on camera, she used the false emphasis that has become common among second-rate newscasters.

I asked her first if we could eliminate the glasses. She said, "Oh no, the producer thinks people won't take me seriously without my glasses." I told her she'd be taken seriously by the way she delivered the news. She removed her glasses and revealed a perfectly beautiful face.

Trained for a total of six hours, she changed her look, her clothing style, and her delivery. She got her anchor job almost immediately afterward and her career has soared. Today she's the host of one of television's most prestigious news programs.

For media appearances, apply the same foolproof

steps you use to prevent nervousness when you give a talk or presentation. Begin with intelligent anticipation. Find out the format of the television or radio program well in advance, how long your segment will be, what time the program will be aired, who else is appearing with you and, most important, who will be interviewing you. The styles of Mike Wallace and Oprah Winfrey are entirely different.

Every PR person or public-relations department in every corporation should have a video cassette library of interview programs so that their clients can study the interviewer's personality, timing, and the style and setting of his interviews before appearing on the show.

Before I appeared on the Tom Snyder program several years ago, I looked at some tapes of his programs. He and his guests sat in big overstuffed wing chairs. That was fine for Tom Snyder—he's six-four, but I'm five-four. I'd have been swallowed up in a chair like that, and I'd lose the look of authority. I called the producer and asked him if he couldn't change the chairs for my interview. No problem at all, he said. The producer gave both of us straight sit-up chairs and both of us looked better.

Prepare your material—well in advance. Six minutes of air time for any kind of television appearance is a lot. On network programs, you'll be on for no more than three to five minutes; local shows, anywhere from eight minutes to half an hour. It doesn't seem like much time, but it's all you need to get your message across.

Say to yourself, This is a million dollars' worth of free advertising time—what ten points do I want to leave with my listener when I go off the air? Write them down and number them so you can count them off on your fingers. Use anecdotes. If you're selling a book, give a few tanta-

lizing tidbits to hook the viewer. Mention the title of your book at least three times.

Go over your points again at the studio while you're in makeup or the green room waiting to go on. Take your notes along when you go into the studio, and put them behind your back. If there's a commercial break, you can take a quick peek at them to refresh your memory.

What do I wear for television?

Women, red puts you ahead. Wear something red. It usually works. However, I was scheduled to appear on the "Today" show several years ago on a Tuesday. I always wear red on TV. At the last minute, they rescheduled me to Thursday. I tuned in to the Tuesday program and saw that every woman on the show that day wore red. I would have been just another one. But on Thursday's show I was the only woman wearing red, so I got camera attention.

Second best for TV is French blue—it's slightly lighter than royal blue and a lovely warm color.

Have a look of dash. Your clothes should be appropriate for television. Film star Nastassia Kinski went on the David Letterman show wearing leather pants and a denim shirt to counteract the class look she'd projected in her previous film. She thought she had dash but it was trash. As she answered the questions, she was fidgeting and squirming.

Her agent called the next day begging me to do something about her image and demeanor before she went on the "Today" show two days later. We got rid of her trash look. She combed her hair back with a bow, and she wore a simple dress. Two days later, she sat quietly with poise and authority, and she came across with her former look of class.

How can I get the TV camera to show me at my best?

When you get to the studio, ask to speak to the floor director. Find out where you're going to sit and which camera will be focused on you. Too often, the tendency in television is to photograph the guest in profile, which is not the most flattering angle. Nor does it help you relate to the listener.

With as much tact and charm as you can muster, request that the camera capture you as full face as possible.

The most frequent television camera shot is the close-up. If you're not among the most photogenic people in the world, your second request is to be photographed from the waist up.

TV lighting men for some unfathomable reason like to highlight the hair. I'd rather have my face interesting than my hair interesting, wouldn't you? Your third request is for what I call burn-out lighting. That's full-front lighting with no shadows on the face.

After President Reagan's first debate with Walter Mondale in the 1984 campaign, Reagan's PR man called to ask me if I had any suggestions. I said the lighting was terrible. It hit Reagan in the chin and the neck, the first place old age comes through loud and clear. One of the things I suggested was to make sure for future television appearances that President Reagan got full-front lighting.

For women of a certain age, remember you can camouflage age-revealing tendons in the neck with a high collar and a dashing pin on one side. Or get to love scarves and use them. They can make a neckline look interesting and flatter your face. Sometimes a chunky necklace can do almost as well.

Do I have to wear special makeup for television?

Don't count on the makeup department in any but the three network stations. Learn to apply makeup for television yourself. You really do have to wear special makeup for TV—it's heavier and masks the flaws better.

Go to a makeup center for help. They'll draw a map of your face that shows you where to apply what. Take it home with you and study it so you can do it yourself. You'll never be dependent on inferior makeup people who don't know your face.

Makeup for men is just as important. Adlai Stevenson and I met in Chicago when he was running for president. We spoke in his office for three hours about what he could do to enhance his image. He was appearing on "Meet the Press" in Washington and invited me to attend.

Nobody had protected him from the ruthlessness of the camera. He was photographed from the side, which made his nose look bigger. He could have enhanced his image if he'd had makeup to minimize his nose, gotten full-front lighting, and been photographed straight on.

Men should always request dark makeup to diminish a double chin. If you're bald, ask for a matte finish for your dome. You want to mask dark circles under your eyes too.

The best advice about men's hair is that it should be well-groomed and make a flattering frame for the face. As I said before, long bangs cover the eyebrows and rob them of expression. Whenever I see a man with hair like that I want to go over and brush it off his face so I can see him. Style your hair close to the hairline and don't let it flop over your forehead.

If you wear glasses but you can see the interviewer without them, don't wear them. They catch the light and detract attention from you. If you appear frequently on camera, find out about the new nonreflecting lenses.

For men, blue's you on television—suit and shirt. No white shirts on television. All the men on a recent Sunday television news program wore blue suits, blue shirts and red ties. They've all heard about red too. This has become their sincere uniform that says, Notice me. Wear a printed tie for a look of distinction and to get away from the uniform.

Cuffs should show about an inch below your sleeves. I learned that from working with Ambassador Sol Linowitz, the chairman of Xerox. I wondered why his hands always looked so graceful. I realized it was the cuffs showing.

Jackets buttoned give you a look of authority. Larry Wachtel, the Prudential-Bache specialist on radio, was a guest on public television's "Wall Street Week." He sat down on the couch and his jacket button popped off. He yelled, "Stop, stop the cameras. Get me a needle and thread. Dorothy Sarnoff says I can't go on television without my coat buttoned."

What do I do to control nerves while waiting to go on?

The production crew is counting down to air time, you're sitting in place, waiting for the red light to go on. Never lean back in the chair. Incline slightly forward, hold your rib cage high, legs crossed at the knees. If you have short thighs, sit with feet on the floor, legs tightly together. In that position, you put everything you've learned about the Sarnoff control of nervousness into action.

With your lips parted, you exhale normally and contract your vital triangle, you're silently mumbling your magic mantra, and you're repeating your opening remarks. This will be your opening no matter what question the interviewer asks you. You're armed with the ten points you want to leave with the listener when you go off the air.

Where do I look when I'm being interviewed on television?

Never look at the camera. When the interviewer turns his attention to you, speak into his eyes. Get your message across to him and it will come across to the viewer.

What if you get a hostile question? How do you keep cool in the hot seat?

When you're asked a hostile question, never register hostility. If you show hostility to your questioner, you lose audience empathy. I learned this when I was singing in nightclubs.

Whenever there was an unruly drunk in the audience, I took the microphone in my hand, focused my attention totally on him and beamed at him with a benevolent face while I was singing. That usually did the trick. With the entire audience looking at him, he shut up.

Don't ever count on your questioner being sympathetic. Be prepared for a grilling. Think beforehand of the ten toughest questions you could get and be ready with your answers. If you can, role-play with someone as the hostile interviewer.

English press baron Roy Thomson of *The Times of London* was grilled by his colleagues for two days to sharpen his answers for a TV interview with Randolph Churchill. "I was glad to appear on radio and television," says Thomson in an article by John May in *International Management.* "A million and a half shares owned by the public kept their value because people liked the straightforwardness of my approach to business and the look of my face."

The look on your face—the benevolent face—is your first defense. It's not a smile, it's a pleasant face that says, Oh, I understand.

Prepare your response while your interviewer is still asking the question. When President Reagan's PR man called me for suggestions after the first Reagan-Mondale debate in 1984, along with the advice about lighting, I proposed that Reagan could eliminate his groping, hesitant sound at the lectern by trying the following technique.

While the questioner is talking, prepare your conclusion. Then think of two or three points that will get you there. The minute the interviewer finishes the question, you begin the answer: first point, second point, third point . . . bingo, your conclusion. It's like a basketball player shooting a basket. Keep your eyes on the basket, and bounce, bounce, bounce, shoot to your conclusion.

When I do radio, I sit down at my place at the table. Unless it's a hanging mike, the microphone is usually about two feet away. The technicians in the control booth take the sound levels with the microphone at that distance. I think the mike that far away from the speaker transmits an impersonal sound. So when the program begins, I pull the mike closer to me and circle it with my arms. This gives my voice a warmer sound, a voice that makes a personal connection with the listener.

So talk to the microphone, not the interviewer on the other side of the table, and you'll embrace the listener with your voice.

REMEMBER

Anticipate intelligently.
Prepare your material.
Have a look of dash.
Check the camera angle, lights.
Prepare ten thoughts you want to leave in the minds of the viewers.
Prepare answers to ten tough questions you hope you won't get.
Say the Sarnoff Mantra.
Do the Sarnoff Squeeze.
Put on the benevolent face.
For radio: Embrace the microphone.

Meetings and Panels: How to Make Them and You Come Off Better

How do I organize a successful panel discussion?

The biggest responsibility in a panel discussion falls to the chairman. When this is your job, follow these steps:

1. Make sure you know three weeks in advance what topic each participant is going to discuss.
2. Advise participants of their time allotment— 170 words on the page equals one minute's talking time. Emphasize that when you say he has ten minutes, you mean ten minutes, not twelve or fifteen or twenty.

3. Have each panelist send in a prepared introduction to himself. This saves you time.
4. Prepare questions for each panelist. Suggest to
   the participants that they come prepared with
   questions for other panelists.
5. Prepare your summation. You need a strong
   conclusion to close the discussion.
6. Two weeks before the event, send out a letter
   to your participants saying you hope they've
   prepared their talks (no one will have) on the
   topic discussed, conforming to the time frame
   you mentioned previously. Tell them you'll
   stick rigidly to the time allotment so they
   should be prepared to stay within it and that a
   prearranged signal will mean the presentation
   should be concluding.

Set the stage for meetings or panel discussions the way
you would for a talk or presentation—to hold listener attention. A small conference room, arranged so participants
sit in semicircles or around a round or oval table, creates
a warmer ambiance.

The format of a panel discussion should be as follows:

You, the chairman, make an opening statement about
what you hope will come out of the discussion. Be certain
you honor your time allotment.

Introduce the panelists.

When each panelist finishes speaking, make a transi-
tion statement that links his discussion with the one following it. Don't question a panelist until all of them have
made their presentations.

As the panelists speak, fill in and modify your final
summation to accommodate their contributions.

When the panelists have finished, try to engage panelist with panelist; encourage the panelists to question each other.

Throw open the session to questions from listeners. It's always a good idea to plant a few questions among friends in the audience to get things started. Cut off long questions or questioners who make speeches by saying, "If I may interpret your comments . . ."

See that all the listeners' questions don't go to the same panelist.

When I spoke at a large conference in Vienna and Connally and Kissinger were on the panel, chaired by Arnold de Borchgrave, Kissinger got all the questions. It turned into a Kissinger show. The chairman never redirected a single question to Connally. He just faded from the scene. He could have registered presence with the audience if he'd asserted himself with questions or added to what had been said.

When the questions from the floor seem to be drying up, make your prepared summation. If you don't prepare a forceful summation and flesh it out as others are presenting, you won't close the panel strongly.

What do I have to know about participating in meetings?

Go to meetings prepared to leave an idea or thought behind that will register strongly with your colleagues. Find out what the meeting's about. Organize your thoughts beforehand or jot them down with a black felt-tip pen while someone else is speaking.

Look eager to get involved in the discussion. Put animation into your face, contract the vital triangle, say the Sarnoff Mantra and your whole persona sends the message, I have something important to say.

How can I communicate authority in a meeting?

The CEO of one of our most prestigious corporations called to consult me about one of the rising stars in his company. He was thirty-nine, handsome—a dazzling smile, a full head of hair, and extremely well dressed—but his demeanor in meetings was holding him back.

The minute he walked into my office, I could see what was wrong. He came in slouched over; it was as though a gray scrim had been pulled over his face.

When I called his attention to the impression he made, he said that in meetings, nothing he hears interests him so he tunes out. That's how he looked—tuned out, detached. No presence.

Using video playback I got him to see the difference that the way you sit in meetings can make. When he sat in the "authority position"—stomach muscles contracted, forearms resting on the edge of the table, hands clasped, he looked like someone in charge. Then we worked to get him to talk eyes up and put "love apples" in his face. He put a red dot on his watch to constantly remind him to use those behaviors that create presence.

Talented and brilliant guys like him think that what they *do* is enough to get them to the top. They don't realize they get there faster if they look and act like leaders.

Where do I look while another person is speaking?

The way you listen in meetings and panel discussions gives messages about you too. Even if you're not talking, you're still on stage. To maintain your presence, listen with interest, focusing your eyes on the speaker. This is focused listening. If he's sitting next to you and he's too close, angle your body in the chair slightly so that you're turned toward him. Animate your face with approval. It says, I'm with you, I'm interested in what you're saying.

Focused listening is crucial when making team presentations. Give full attention to your fellow presenter and you help him sell. This contributes to your colleague's authority and your team's impact.

I attended a Partners in Medicine dinner and panel discussion recently. One of the principal speakers positioned himself about two feet *behind* the speaker's dais to speak. None of the people sitting on the dais knew what to do. They didn't want to turn their backs on the audience to focus on him, so they just stared vacantly out at the audience. This was terribly distracting. In this kind of situation, angle your chair and turn your body in profile to focus on the speaker.

What should I do with my hands while I'm talking or listening at a table during a meeting or panel discussion?

Remember, fidgeting with your fingers, pushing back your cuticles, playing with a pen or paperclip distracts the listener and detracts from you. To keep hands under control, clasp your hands and rest your forearms on the table edge, midway between your wrist and your elbow. Automatically you sit up straighter in your chair. Your bearing says, I know that I know.

REMEMBER

Organize a panel discussion in advance.
Prepare the guidelines for each participant.
Control the timing of the speakers.
Stimulate discussion.
Focus on the speakers.
Prepare introductions and summaries in advance.

Social Ease

What makes people shy?

Recently the *New York Times* noted that social anxiety is the single most common psychological problem, affecting as many as 40 percent of adults, studies have found. At a party with strangers, for instance, three-quarters of adults feel anxiety.

The actress Ann-Margret professes publicly to being shy. When an interviewer asked her why she was shy, she answered, "It's not easy when I'm me."

I think that's why I became an actress. I was so painfully shy that in college if I knew the answer to the professor's question and raised my hand, I blocked when he called on me and couldn't get the answer out. In social situations in later life I would freeze. But playing another character on stage, I owned the world. I wasn't playing me.

"The best estimate is that 40 percent of all Americans suffer from shyness," says Philip G. Zimbardo, professor of social psychology at Stanford University. This group includes Barbara Walters, athlete Terry Bradshaw, Woody Allen and Carol Burnett.

What is shyness?

Shyness is I-ness. Shyness is really wondering if you have other people's approval. Man's number-one need is survival. His second is approval.

For some people, shyness can be painful because of anxiety in social situations that wouldn't bother other people—like asking a stranger for the time or a waiter to take back an undercooked steak. When I was a child I was at a concert with my mother. She wanted me to ask the woman sitting next to me if we could borrow her program for a moment. I couldn't do it.

How can I prevent being nervous when I meet people in social situations?

Prepare. Preparation for any communicating situation is a must. You've been invited to a big dinner party in two weeks. You know that one of the other guests is a politician. Scan the newspapers and magazines; listen to television or radio newscasts for topics of conversation in political areas.

Pretend you're an interviewer on a talk show. Think of some questions to ask that can't be answered yes or no. "In your opinion, who . . ." "How do you suppose . . ." "What do you think of . . ." Keep the momentum going. I always say I'd rather have good conversation with dinner than wine.

Is there anything I can do to overcome shyness?

People react differently to their shyness. Some are so afraid of looking foolish that they'll do anything to avoid situations that make them vulnerable to other people's judgments. Other people get through the social occasions that terrify them, but the toll it takes in anxiety and physical suffering—shallow breathing, palpitating heart, shaking hands—is enormous.

A few people perform so effectively that their shyness is not perceived by others. Drugs, psychiatrists, psychologists, even hypnotists treat people for nervousness and social phobias. When the therapies and tranquilizers and gimmicks prescribed to fend off fear and anxiety don't work, people come to me.

The chairman of a large financial company, an ex-marine and Rhodes Scholar, confessed to his friend Jock Elliott, chairman emeritus of Ogilvy & Mather, that he envied Elliott's ease at the lectern. "I taught public speaking in the marines," he told Elliott, "but I'm so frightened at having to get up and give a talk that I haven't done it for ten years." He had been in analysis for nine years and still couldn't do it. Jock told him, "Go to Dorothy Sarnoff. I think she can help you."

He came for one two-hour session on a Monday, another two-hour session on Tuesday, and another on Wednesday. On Friday he gave a talk at MIT. After it was over he ran to the telephone to call me. "Why'd I have to spend ten years of my life in hell when you got me over it in four hours?"

I've also helped people who find any social situation or just coping with life itself too much for them. A while back, *Reader's Digest* published an article about my three steps to self-confidence. One of the editors called to ask if I might be able to help his sister. She was fifty-seven years old when her husband left her. She went into shock and wasn't able to talk. She'd been going to a psychiatrist for three years for her depression but it hadn't helped her.

She came to my office. I said to her, "If you go to the grocery, what would you buy?" She couldn't answer. There was a watercolor on the wall over my desk. It was a scene of a town square in Havana, Cuba, on a stormy day, palm trees swept by the wind, dark clouds hanging menacingly overhead; I asked her what came to mind when she looked at the picture. "Storm, clouds, angry . . ." she said and the words started to come. Four weeks later, after five more hours, she was the mistress of ceremonies at her sister's wedding anniversary.

The difference between my approach and a psychiatrist's approach is that psychiatrists concentrate on why you do something, while I concentrate on what you can do about it. A client who's the publisher of one of Rupert Murdoch's magazines told me, "When I come to you I feel like I'm going to my psychiatrist, except that you understand me better." Why lie on the couch for years to find out why you have a fear when in twenty-four hours you can do something about it?

I got a call one morning from a woman in New Orleans. She told me that she and her husband had read my first book and had made plans to come with their four children to work with me. Four months later, her husband was killed. "I'm bringing those children to New York to see you," she said. "It's what my husband would have wanted."

We scheduled an early morning appointment. I arrived at my office to find her waiting outside my door. She was clearly in shock—worn out, limp, she could barely talk. She told me that her son, age twenty, was caving in under the pressure of having to act as father of the family. None of his three sisters paid any attention to him. The youngest of her daughters was fourteen and had become uncontrollable, coming home late, not doing her home-work. "I'm bringing them all in tomorrow."

I replayed the videotape of our conversation for her. She looked at herself on the screen and said, "No wonder my children don't listen to me. Who'd want to be around a mother like that?"

She came back the next afternoon with her whole family. She'd put on makeup; she was even standing taller and straighter. I sat everybody down around a table—a round table, of course—turned on the video camera and said to the boy, "What do you say to Laurie when she goes out?" "I say, be home by ten, but at eleven-thirty she still isn't home." He didn't look her in the eyes. He was casual and didn't seem to mean what he said.

I replayed the videotape. "Laurie knows you don't mean business," I told him. "Look her in the eye and say it as though you mean it." I demonstrated. He tried it.

After a two-hour session, they all went back to New Orleans. A few weeks later the woman called to tell me that Laurie was coming home at night when she was supposed to, and the child's attitude had changed from rebellious to cooperative.

How can I keep my palms from perspiring when I shake hands in social situations?

I always make a point of shaking hands with new clients. Handshakes communicate messages. A limp or wet hand-shake makes a negative impression. Do the Sarnoff Squeeze for the physical control of nervousness and say your Sarnoff Mantra . . . I'm glad I'm here, I'm glad you're here . . . for the mental control of nervousness. As you walk into an introduction situation your handshake will be dry.

You want a firm but not bone-crushing handshake. At receptions at the Department of State, Secretary of State George Shultz had to stand and shake hands with hundreds of people. On such occasions he has his arm in a sling and his hand in a brace with only two fingers showing to protect himself from overvigorous handshakers. He touches the other person's hand gently, then turns his palm up and passes the guest's hand to the next person in line to move the guest along.

How can I sound friendly and not nervous when people call on the telephone?

One of Nelson Rockefeller's writers had a friend who never appeared in public without her false eyelashes. She called her one morning. The writer said, "Lillian, you don't have your eyelashes on yet, do you?" Lillian said, "How did you know?" The writer said, "I can tell by the tone of your voice."

Tone is very important on the telephone. Your tone should be personal no matter what the words. So contract the vital triangle, mumble the Sarnoff Mantra and put a warm hello in your caller's name by the way you say it. You'll sound like an instant friend.

REMEMBER

Social situations are more fun if you prepare for them.

Use the attitude adjustment mantra.

Never Be Nervous Again!

In this book I've given you a foolproof formula for the mental and physical control of nervousness. It's the same technique I teach my clients in seminars and in private sessions.

Remember the ten steps of the Sarnoff Method:

1. Prepare with intelligent anticipation.
2. Get all the information you can about the speaking situation.
3. Organize, write and edit your material.
4. Prepare fast food for the eyes at the lectern.
5. Familiarize, don't memorize your talk.
6. Create the look of authority.
7. Set the scene for listener attention.
8. Adjust your attitude with the Sarnoff Mantra.
9. Prevent butterflies with the Sarnoff Squeeze.
10. Be in control in any situation.

You're never too young or too old to improve the way you communicate, no matter what you do. With the Sarnoff Method you won't wonder or doubt. You'll know you won't look ridiculous to others. You'll present yourself with confidence and authority in any communicating situation—professional, social and domestic. (Even family life requires communication skills.)

Use these antinervousness techniques to ask for a raise, make a sale, cope with a family crisis, feel comfortable in social and business situations, campaign for office, deal with hostile interviews.

The Sarnoff Method eliminates the negative and accentuates the positive. It shields you from negative feelings so that your mind and body chemistry stay positive. No more nervousness.

The Sarnoff Method Can Change Your Life

"Dorothy Sarnoff is a magician," says a rare-book dealer who's become a national figure in her profession and is invited to speak all over the world since learning the Sarnoff Method.

She gave her son a Sarnoff seminar for his high-school graduation present. He's become an exchange student at Oxford University and captain of the Oxford debate team —unheard of for an American. "I was chosen," he writes, "on the basis of my smooth presentation style."

"As you can see from the letterhead," writes John R. McKernan, Jr., the governor of Maine, "my campaign for governor last fall was successful. Needless to say, the Sarnoff Method gave me a lot more confidence in maintaining a natural approach to public appearances."

"I went through the ordeal of making my Maiden Speech in the House of Lords yesterday," writes Lord

Derwent, the former Robin Johnstone of N. M. Rothschild and Sons in London. "I came through with flying colors, thanks to the Sarnoff technique."

"There have been kings and presidents who would have paid highly for the wisdom contained in the Sarnoff Method," writes a corporate executive. "It's given me the encouragement to speak truthfully and to reach for the soul of my audience."

"How great a difference the Sarnoff Method has made to our lives," writes the U.S. ambassador to Egypt. "I couldn't have survived the last decade without it. I've never felt at a loss or uneasy before an audience, in front of a camera, or at a dinner table since learning the Sarnoff antinervousness formula. More than technique, I learned style, self-confidence and grace."

You, too, have the power within you to become a forceful, persuasive, confident communicator. Master the simple principles set out in this book and you will **NEVER BE NERVOUS AGAIN.**

Appendix:
A Speech by William Safire, Openings and Closings, Quotes and Anecdotes

Here is a speech by the brilliant *New York Times* columnist William Safire, loaded with wisdom and excellent advice.

William Safire: 1978 Commencement Address

Classmates: I entered this university with the Class of '51, and am finally receiving my degree with the Class of '78. There is hope for slow learners.

We have not heard an eloquent speech out of the White House in a long time. Why? When you ask the speechwriters of Mr. Ford and Mr. Carter, they give you this explanation: They say that "high-flown rhetoric" is not their man's style.

But that is not responsive. A flowery speech is a bad speech. Simple, straight English prose can be used to build a great speech. There has to be a more profound reason for the reluctance of the presidents of the seventies to write out their thoughts plainly and deliver them in words we can all understand.

If you press the president's aides—and that's my job, to press them hard—they'll admit that their man much prefers to ad-lib answers to questions. He's not good at what they call a "set" speech.

What do they really mean by that? They mean that a speech—a written speech, developing an idea—is not what people want to hear. People prefer short takes, Q

155

and A; the attention span of most Americans on serious matters is about twenty seconds, the length of a television clip.

In the same way, people do not want to read articles as they once did; today, if you cannot get it in a paragraph, forget it.

As a result, we're becoming a short-take society. Our presidency, which Theodore Roosevelt called a "bully pulpit," is a forum for thirty-second spots. Our food for thought is junk food.

What has brought this about? I don't blame President Carter for this—he reflects the trend, he did not start it. I don't flail out at the usual whipping-boy, television. And I'm not suggesting that there isn't plenty of excellent writing being published.

The reason for the decline of the written word—written speeches, written articles—is that we, as a people, are writing less and talking more. Because it takes longer to prepare your thoughts on paper, that means we are ad-libbing more, and it means we are thinking more superficially. An ad lib has its place, but not ad nauseam.

That's one of those sweeping statements that pundits are permitted to make. But let me turn reporter for a minute and prove to you that we're talking more and writing less.

Most people are not writing personal letters any more. Oh, the volume of first-class letters has doubled since 1950, but here's the way the mail breaks down. Over 80 percent is business-related; over 10 percent is greeting card, and Christmas card; and only 3 percent is from one person to another to chew the fat.

More and more, we're relying on commercial poets and cartoonists to express our thoughts for us. Tomorrow is Mother's Day; how many of us are relying on canned sentiments? I remember my brother once laboriously handmade a card for my mother: on the front was "I'll never forget you Mother," and inside it said "You gave away my dog." Okay, he was sore, but at least he was original.

The greatest cultural villain of our times, in my opinion, has a motherly image: Ma Bell. The telephone company. Instead of writing, people are calling; instead of communicating, they're staying in touch.

Here we are, all now holders of college degrees. When was the last time you wrote, or received, a long, thoughtful letter? When was the last time you wrote a passionate love letter? No, that takes time, effort, thought—there's a much easier way, the telephone. The worst insult is when kids call home, collect, for money; when my kids go to college, the only way they'll get a nickel out of me is to write for it.

As the percentage of personal mail has dwindled, the number of telephone installations since 1950 has quadrupled. What has undermined the average person's need to write is simple economics: While the cost of a letter has gone up, the cost of a call has gone down.

During World War I, a first-class letter cost two cents an ounce; in a few months, it will be fifteen cents an ounce. In that same sixty years, a New York to San Francisco call has gone from twenty dollars for three minutes down to fifty-three cents today, if you're willing to call at night or on a weekend. Letters up 800 percent; phone calls down to one-fortieth of the cost to grandpa. No wonder the market share of communication has dropped for writers. In the year I was a freshman here, the postal service had over a third of the communication business; today, it is one-sixth, and falling.

And it's going to get worse. Phonevision is on the way.

We have seen what happened to the interpersonal correspondence of love in the past generation. The purple passages of prose and tear-stained pages of the love letter have become the heavy breathing, grunts, and "Like, I mean, y'know wow" of the love call. The next stage, with the visual dimension, requires not even a loud sigh: we can just wave at each other to say hello; wiggle our fingers to express affection; raise our eyebrows to ask "what's new," get a shrug in reply, and sign off with a smile and a wink.

We need not degenerate further from written English to verbal signals to sign language. We need to become modern reactionaries; I consider myself a neo-Neanderthal, and my happiest moment of the year comes as daylight saving ends in October, when I can turn back the clock.

How do we save ourselves from the tyranny of the telephone? How do we liberate our language from the addiction to the ad lib?

If this were an off-the-cuff presentation, I would drift off into a fuzzy evasion like "There are no easy answers." But one thing I have learned in preparing my first commencement address, and the main advice I shall burden you with today, is this: There are plenty of easy answers. The big trick is to think about them and write them down.

There are four steps to the salvation of the English language, and thus to the rejuvenation of clear thinking in your working lives.

First, remember that first drafts are usually stupid. If you shoot off your mouth with your first draft—that is, if you make your presentation orally—your stupidity shines forth for all to hear. But if you write your first draft—of a letter, a memo, a description of some transcendental experience that comes to you while jogging—then you fall on your face in absolute privacy. You get the chance to change it all around. It is harder to put your foot in your mouth when you have your pen in your hand.

Second, reject the notion that honesty and candor demand that you "let it all hang out." That's not honesty, that's intellectual laziness. Tuck some of it in; edit some of it out. Talking on your feet, spinning thoughts off the top of your head, just rapping along in a laid-back way has been glorified as expressing your natural self. But you did not get an education to become natural, you got an education to become civilized. Composition is a discipline; it forces us to think. If you want to "get in touch with your feelings," fine—talk to yourself, we all do. But if you want to communicate with another thinking human being, get in touch with your thoughts. Put them in order; give them a purpose; use them to persuade, to instruct, to discover, to seduce. The secret way to do this is to write it down, and then cut out the confusing parts.

Third, never forget that you own the telephone, the telephone does not own you. Most people cannot bear to listen to a phone ring without answering it. It's easy to not answer a letter, but it's hard to not answer a phone. Let me pass along a solution that has changed my life. When I was in the Nixon Administration, my telephone was tapped (I had been associating with known journalists). So I took an interest in the instrument itself. Turn it upside down; you will notice a lever that says "louder." Turn it away from the direction of louder. That is the direction of emancipation. If somebody needs to see you, they'll come over. If somebody needs to tell you what they think, or even express how they feel, they can write. There are those who will call you a recluse, a hermit—but it is better to listen to your own different drummer than to go through life with a ringing in your ears.

My fourth point will impress upon you the significance

of the written word. Those of you who have been secretly taking notes, out of a four-year habit, will recall that I spoke of "four steps" to the salvation of the English language. Here it is: There is no fourth step. I had four steps in mind when I began, but I forgot it. Now, if I were ad-libbing, I would remember I had promised four points, and I would do what so many stump speakers do—toss in the all-purpose last point, which usually begins "There are no easy answers." But in writing down what you think, you can go back and fix it—instead of having to phumph around with a phony fourth point, you can change your introduction to "There are three steps." Perhaps you wonder why I did not do so. Not out of any excess of honesty, or unwillingness to make a simple fix—I just wanted you to see the fourth step take shape before your very eyes.

Is the decline of the written word inevitable? Will the historians of the future deal merely in oral history? I hope not. I hope that oral history will limit itself to the discovery of toothpaste and the invention of mouthwash. I don't want to witness the de-composing of the art of composition, or be present when we get in touch with our feelings and lose contact with our minds.

I'm a conservative in politics, which means I believe that we as a people have to lead our leaders, to show them how we want to be led.

Accordingly, I think we have to send a message to the podium from the audience: We're ready for more than Q and A. We're ready for five or ten minutes of sustained explication. A fireside chat will not turn out our fires. If you will take the time to prepare, we are prepared to pay attention.

That, of course, is contrary to the trend, against the grain. It can only come from people who care enough to compose, who get in the habit of reading rather than listening, of being in communication instead of only in contact.

When Great Britain was fighting World War II alone, an American president did something that would be considered cornball today: FDR sent Churchill a poem, along with a letter, that said:

> Sail on, O Ship of State!
> Sail on O Union, strong and great!
> Humanity with all its fears,
> With all the hopes of future years,
> Is hanging breathless on thy fate!

Churchill took the message from Wendell Willkie, who brought FDR's letter, and selected a poem in answer. At that moment, looking east, England faced invasion; looking to the west across the Atlantic, Churchill saw potential help. The poem he sent concluded:

> And not by eastern windows only,
> When daylight comes,
>   comes in the light;
> In front, the sun climbs slow,
>   how slowly,
> But westward, look,
>   the land is bright.

High-flown rhetoric? Perhaps. And perhaps poetry, which had an honored place in a 1961 inauguration, is too rich for some tastes today.

And now I remember the fourth step. I like to think we can demand some sense of an occasion, some uplift, some inspiration from our leaders. Not empty words and phony promises—but words full of meaning, binding thoughts together with purpose, holding promise of understandable progress. If we ask for it, we'll get it—if we fail to ask, we'll get more Q and A.

I believe we can arrest the decline of the written word, thereby achieving a renaissance of clarity. And not by Eastern Establishment windows only, but this side of the Potomac, the Charles and the Hudson Rivers—"Westward, look, the land is bright."

Openings and Closings

Anecdotes and quotations make for attention-getting openings, memorable closings, and colorful point makers throughout your talks (and conversation). Following are some anecdotes clients have used that can be adapted to your needs.

Where there is no credit,
the quote is anonymous.

Discovery:
Thomas Edison was mocked for trying some twelve hundred materials for the filament of his great dream, the incandescent light bulb. "You have failed twelve hundred times," said a regimented thinker of that day. "I have not failed," countered Edison. "I have discovered twelve hundred materials that won't work."

162

For an opening, add: Like Edison, our company is constantly experimenting and discovering new products . . . that *do* work. Today I'd like to tell you about some of our most recent and impressive ones.

For a closing, add: We have not failed, either. We have succeeded in eliminating all the impossibilities. Now we will succeed in finding the possibilities . . . the answers to our problems.

Reality:

A mother was having difficulty in waking her son. He pulled the covers over his head. "I'm not going to school," he said, "I'm not ever going to school again." "Are you sick?" "No, I'm sick of school. They hate me. They call me names. They make fun of me. Why should I go?" "I can give you two good reasons," the mother replied. "The first is you're forty-two years old and the second is you're the principal."

For an opening, add: None of us can hide under the covers. We must all face reality . . . the reality of the problem confronting our community.

For a closing, add: We are not going to hide under the covers any longer. Together we will face the problem confronting our community. Together we will win.

Skill:

The situation we're facing here reminds me of the time the generator failed in a small town. The city was plunged into darkness and the president of the utility company tried everything to restore the power and failed. Finally, in despair, he called a professor of engineering from the local college. The fellow walked in, assessed the situation, gave the generator a single tap, and ... on went the lights!

The professor sent a bill for $1,001 the following day. Puzzled, the president of the utility company called him and said, "I don't understand your bill." The professor replied, "Oh, that's easy: one dollar for tapping, one thousand dollars for knowing *where* to tap."

For an opening, add: We have a major problem in our industry. To find the best solution, we must find out "where to tap." That's what I want to speak with you about today.

For a closing, add: Like the professor, our real value to the industry lies in our know-how ... and *we know how*. Let's "tap" our resources. Let's make them work for us.

Direction:

Our situation today is much like that of Oliver Wendell Holmes, who once found himself on a train and couldn't locate his ticket. While the conductor watched, Justice Holmes searched through all his pockets in vain. The conductor, recognizing Holmes, said, "Don't worry, you don't need your ticket, you'll probably find it when you get off the train. Just mail it back to the Pennsylvania Railroad." With irritation, the Justice replied, "My dear sir, the problem is *not* 'Where is my ticket?' The problem is, 'Where am I going?' " And that is the question haunting Main Street, Wall Street and Pennsylvania Avenue. Where are we going?

The presence of this wonderful group of company executives here today proves that you don't have to be in *Who's Who* to know What's What.

Returning:
In his novel titled *You Can't Go Home Again,* Thomas
Wolfe went to great lengths—over nine hundred pages,
in fact—to prove his point. I am here this morning to
disprove it and tell you it's great to be home again! You'll
be relieved to know that my message is a great deal
shorter than Wolfe's.

Brevity:
My talk will be less than sixteen minutes. Here's what
keeps me in line, when it comes to time limits. A clergyman was asked to give the baccalaureate address at Yale.
The chapel was full when he began. He had a theme for
each letter in the university's name. He took twenty minutes to talk about Y, as in Youth. He took nearly eighteen
minutes to talk about A, as in Activism. Twenty-two minutes were devoted to L, as in Loyalty. And, although people were leaving in droves, he continued for almost
another eighteen minutes discussing E, as in Energy.

When he finally finished, one solitary student was
kneeling in the practically empty chapel. The clergyman
walked over, and asked if he was praying. "Yes Reverend,
I'm giving a prayer of thanks." "For what, son?" "I'm
giving thanks that I'm graduating from Yale . . . and not
the Massachusetts Institute of Technology!"
—*Robert M. Price*

Decisions:
Whenever I begin to give a speech, I feel somewhat in-
adequate when I think of the speeches I have heard given
by my very special friend, Clark Clifford. In fact I have
heard him tell a story about his friend Jim Forestal, who
had just gotten out of college and had gone with an in-

vestment banking firm. There was a man on Wall Street at that time who was having spectacular success and Jim hoped that he might meet him sometime and learn something from him. And he did meet him at a reception, and steered him off to one side and said, "Sir, I'm just beginning my career. I wonder if I might ask you some questions." The man said, "Of course." Jim said, "First, what is the secret to your success?" And the man said, "Making the right decisions." Well, Jim thought, that helped some. "And," Jim said, "how do you get to the point where you can make the right decisions?" The man said, "Experience." "Now," Jim said, "my last question is, how do you get the experience?" And the man said, "Making the wrong decisions."

—Harry A. Jacobs, Jr.

Marketing:

Marketing today is a lot like surfing. Consumers around the world create the wave, and the marketing people ride it. If we understand how the wave is formed—if we wax our boards thoroughly and keep a firm footing—then we're in for the ride of our lives.

If, on the other hand, we enter the water in a state of innocence, we're likely to miss the wave completely, or catch just a part of it, or fall off, and maybe even be swept under.

One thing is certain: the potential for loss or gain lies with us in marketing. The consumer wave is flowing and growing now, and it'll continue to do so, with or without us.

—Jerry Pickholz

Objectives:

You may recall that Willie Sutton, the famous bank robber, when asked why he robbed banks, replied, logically

166

enough, "Because that's where the money is." Well, corporations will be doing more for society simply because, increasingly, "that's where the money is."

—*Louis V. Gerstner, Jr.*

Duck hunters tell us that the way to hit a target is to aim where it's going to be, not to where it's been. It is clear to me that corporations must aim their strategic planning at where those moving targets are going to be.

Autobiography:

My great-grandfather, the first Robert Wood Johnson, was born on a Pennsylvania farm in 1845. One account says he left the farm because it was the only one in the region that hadn't struck coal. At about the time of the Civil War he went to Poughkeepsie, New York, to begin an apprenticeship in pharmacy . . . modern medicine was then in its infancy.

Then, in 1876, the year of the nation's hundredth birthday, my great grandfather went to the centennial celebration in Philadelphia. There he listened to a lecture by the noted English surgeon, Sir Joseph Lister. Lister was advancing his theory that wound contamination from invisible micro-organisms was responsible for the deaths of untold numbers of surgical patients. Many doubted Dr. Lister's theories—Robert Wood Johnson was not one of them.

In 1886 he came to New Brunswick with his two brothers and began the Johnson & Johnson business.

—*Robert Wood Johnson, IV*

The Power of the Press

People in public life have an intimate understanding of what has come to be known as "The Power of the Press" in this country. My own fascination with this subject goes back to high school, when we were studying the Spanish-American War. There was a story of how William Randolph Hearst recruited the famous American artist, Frederick Remington, and sent him off to Cuba to do some sketches of the civil strife in that country that promised to lead to war. After arriving in Cuba and searching in vain for anything dramatic to sketch, Remington cabled Hearst, "Everything is quiet. There's no trouble here. There will be no war. Wish to return." To which Hearst replied: "Please remain, Remington. You furnish the pictures and I'll furnish the war."

—*Steve Ward*

Closing:

What keeps a magazine—or a human being, for that matter—contemporary? Fads come and go, events occur and are forgotten, but home and family and justice and religion and love of country stay on always. These are the blocks to build on. These are the factors that are forever contemporary. Speaking of forever, I suspect that's how long some of you think I've been talking. So I'll take this opportunity to thank you for your attention and to sit down while I myself am still contemporary.

—*John Mack Carter*

Freedom:

"If you knew what freedom was," Herodotus quotes a Greek saying to a Persian, "you would fight for it with bare hands if you had no weapons." You graduates know what freedom is. So do all you can in your lives to improve the world, but beware of the ruthless and the unquestioning. The promise of America, which you can now inherit as educated citizens, is that bread and justice can be

and you have a nice time. Now don't you think it's only right that once a week you should go to God's house, just for one hour?"

The boy thought it over and said, "But Mom, what would you think if you were invited to somebody's house and every time you went, the fellow was never there?"

Absence makes the heart go wander.

Action
There is no genius in life like the genius of energy and activity.
—Donald G. Mitchell

Action may not always bring happiness; but there's no happiness without action.
—Disraeli

Iron rusts from disuse; water loses its purity from stagnation and in cold weather becomes frozen; even so does inaction sap the vigors of the mind.
—Leonardo da Vinci

Never mistake motion for action.
—Ernest Hemingway

Addiction
I take it to be a principal rule of life, not to be too much addicted to only one thing.
—Terence

Advertising
Advertising may be described as the science of arresting the human intelligence long enough to get money from it.

171

Advertisements contain the only truths to be relied on in a newspaper.

—*Thomas Jefferson*

Advice

By the time a man asks you for advice, he has generally made up his mind what he wants to do, and is looking for confirmation rather than counseling.

—*Sydney J. Harris*

Age

Adolescence is a period of rapid change. Between the ages of fifteen and seventeen a parent can age as much as twenty years.

In youth we learn; in age we understand.

—*Marie Ebner-Eschenbach*

Ambition

All ambitions are lawful except those which climb upward on the miseries or credulities of mankind.

—*Joseph Conrad*

The rung of a ladder was never meant to rest upon, but only to hold a man's foot to enable him to put the other one somewhat higher.

—*Thomas Huxley*

Anger

Two things a man should never be angry at: what he can help and what he cannot help.

—*Thomas Fuller*

172

Anger is not only inevitable, it is necessary. Its absence means indifference, the most disastrous of human failings.
—*Arthur Ponsonby*

You raise your voice when you should reinforce your argument.

Apologizing
Nine times out of ten, the first thing a man's companion knows of his shortcomings is from his apology.
—*Oliver Wendell Holmes*

Appeal
Frank Weil, a lawyer, was playing golf with Danny Kaye and hit the ball out of bounds. He had to take another shot. This time he hit it right down the fairway—perfect shot. Danny Kaye said, "You always were better on appeals."

Appearance
Her features didn't seem to know the value of teamwork.
—*George Ade*

Approval
Applause is the only appreciated interruption.
—*Arnold Glasow*

A man cannot be comfortable without his own approval.
—*Mark Twain*

Appreciation is a wonderful thing; it makes what is excellent in others belong to us as well.
—*Voltaire*

I can live for two months on a good compliment.
—*Mark Twain*

The deepest principle in human nature is craving to be appreciated.

—*William James*

Arrogance

Early in life I had to choose between arrogance and hypocritical humility. I chose honest arrogance and have seen no occasion to change.

—*Frank Lloyd Wright*

Art

A man who works with his hands is a laborer; a man who works with his hands and his brain is a craftsman; but a man who works with his hands, his brain and his heart is an artist.

When love and skill work together, expect a masterpiece.

—*John Ruskin*

Attention

If I have ever made any valuable discoveries, it has been owing more to patient attention, than to any other talent.

—*Isaac Newton*

The art of acting consists of keeping people from coughing.

—*Sir Ralph Richardson*

Attitude

Our attitudes control our lives; attitudes are a secret power working twenty-four hours a day, for good or bad.

It is of paramount importance that we know how to harness and control this great force.

—*Charles Simmons*

When you get to the end of your rope, tie a knot and hang on.

—*Franklin D. Roosevelt*

Authority

Somebody jested with a noted British jurist, Lord Salisbury, saying that the bishop was a man of greater authority than he. "A judge can do no more than say, 'You be hanged.' A bishop has the power to say, 'You be damned.' "

"That may be true," said Salisbury, "but when a judge says, 'You be hanged,' you *are* hanged!"

Boredom

A bore is someone who deprives you of solitude without providing you with company.

—*Gian Vincenzo Gravina*

A yawn is a silent shout.

—*G. K. Chesterton*

Breeding

Good breeding consists in concealing how much we think of ourselves and how little we think of the other person.

—*Mark Twain*

Brevity

There is much to be said for not saying much.

—*Frank Tyger*

Business

Business is a combination of war and sport.

—*Andre Maurois*

Few people do business well who do nothing else.

—*Lord Chesterton*

Busy

Busy people have no time to be busybodies.

—*Austin O'Malley*

Campaigning

You campaign in poetry, you govern in prose.

—*Mario Cuomo*

Celebrity

The nice thing about being a celebrity is that when you bore people they think it's their fault.

—*Henry Kissinger*

Change

After the death of her father, my friend tried to persuade her eighty-year-old mother to move in with her. The older woman was adamant: "No! Absolutely no! I've always said that I'd never live with any of my kids. I've seen too many problems arise from that kind of situation." My friend said, "Yes, Mom, but you're different." "I know I am," replied her mother, "but you're not."

There is a certain relief in change, even though it be from bad to worse; as I have found traveling in a stage-coach, that it is often a comfort to shift one's position and be bruised in a new place.

—*Washington Irving*

176

Character

How a man plays the game shows something of his character; how he loses it shows all of it.

—*Camden County, Georgia,* Tribune

Charisma

If we get charisma in a president, as in F.D.R. or J.F.K., let's be grateful. But far more important is "gravitas," which connotes moral leadership and the capacity to grow in competence.

—*Lehoren Arisian*

Charm

Charm is having such a glow within you that you cast a becoming light on others.

—Vogue

Children

Children are a comfort in your old age, but like Social Security, not nearly as much as you had expected.

—*Robert Orbin*

The first half of our lives is ruined by our parents and the second half by our children.

—*Clarence Darrow*

Children aren't happy with nothing to ignore. That's what parents were created for.

—*Ogden Nash*

Choice

We inherit our relatives and our features and may not escape them; but we can select our clothing and our friends, and let us be careful that both fit us.

—*Volney Streamer*

Choices

Between two evils, I always pick the one I never tried before.

—Mae West

Choice has always been a privilege of those who could afford to pay for it.

—Ellen Frankfort

We are all ready to be savage in some cause. The difference between a good man and a bad one is the choice of the cause.

—William James

Civilization

The end of the human race will be that it will eventually die of civilization.

—Ralph Waldo Emerson

The salvation of mankind lies only in making everything the concern of all.

—Aleksandr Solzhenitsyn

College

I recall the response of Charles Eliot, a former Harvard president, when he was congratulated for making Harvard a "storehouse of knowledge." He said, "I scarcely deserve the credit. It is simply that the freshmen bring so much knowledge in, and the seniors take so little out."

Commencement speakers

A commencement speaker serves the same purpose as the body at an Irish wake. It's essential to have one, but you don't expect it to say anything.

—Mario Cuomo

Committees

When Lindbergh landed at Orly Field after his solo trans-atlantic flight, there were huge crowds applauding him and lots of reporters waiting to interview him. They asked him if it had been a difficult experience. He said, "Oh no, I did it alone."

A committee is a group that keeps minutes and loses hours.

—Milton Berle

The ideal committee consists of two, four or six people who haven't time, and one person who likes to run things his own way.

Kearny, Nebraska, Hub

Competition

There were two hunters in the woods. They came around a bend and there facing them, only a few yards away, was a huge grizzly bear. One of the hunters reached into his knapsack, pulled out a pair of sneakers and hastily started putting them on. The other hunter said, "What are you doing that for? You can't outrun a grizzly." The first hunter said, "I don't have to outrun the grizzly, I only have to outrun *you.*"

—President Ronald Reagan
(quoted by Jock Elliott)

If a competitor is doing it, it must be good.

—Robert Half

Computers

I can't remember what excuses folks gave for their mistakes before there were computers.

—Frank Clark

179

Concern

The concern for man and his destiny must always be the chief interest of all technical effort.

—Albert Einstein

Confidence

No one can make you feel inferior without your consent.

—Eleanor Roosevelt

One of the very best of all earthly possessions is self-possession.

—George D. Prentice

Confidence is that feeling by which the mind embarks on great and honorable courses with a sure hope and trust in itself.

—Cicero

The easiest kind of relationship for me is with ten thousand people. The hardest is with one.

—Joan Baez

I begin to understand that the promises of the world are, for the most part, vain phantoms, and that to have faith in oneself and become something of worth and value is the best and safest course.

—Michelangelo

Four be the things I'd been better without: Love, curiosity, freckles, and doubt.

—Dorothy Parker

Connections

Many a live wire would be a dead one if it weren't for his connections.

—Wilson Mizner

Conscience

Conscience is that still small voice that says somebody may be watching.

—*George Shultz*

Conventions

The trouble with conventions is that I expand my waist-line as well as my mind.

Conversation

A good conversationalist is not one who remembers what was said, but says what someone wants to remember.

—*John Mason Brown*

Conversation is but carving;
Give no more to every guest
Than he's able to digest,
Give him always of the prime,
And by a little at a time;
Give to all but just enough,
Let them neither starve nor stuff
And that each may have his due,
Let your neighbour carve for you.

—*Sir Walter Scott*

Blessed are they who have nothing to say, and who cannot be persuaded to say it.

—*James Russell Lowell*

Half the world is composed of people who have something to say and can't, and the other half who have nothing to say and keep saying it.

—*Robert Frost*

It wasn't just Eliza Doolittle's Cockney accent that done 'er in: She 'ad nothing to say.

Nothing lowers the level of conversation more than raising the voice.

—Stanley Horowitz

Conviction
The difference between a conviction and a prejudice is that you can explain a conviction without getting angry.

—Reader's Digest

Courage
A great deal of talent is lost in the world for want of a little courage.

—Sidney Smith

Courage is the first of human qualities because it is the quality which guarantees all others.

—Winston Churchill

Fear nothing, for every renewed effort raises all former failures into lessons, all sins into experience.

—Katherine Tingley

Cowardice
To sin by silence when they should protest makes cowards out of men.

—Abraham Lincoln

Creativity
Creativity is the act of bringing something new into the world, whether a symphony, a novel, a supermarket or a

new casserole. It is based first on communication with oneself, then testing that communication with experience and reality.

—*S. I. Hayakawa*

Deception

It ain't so much what folks don't know as what they know that ain't so.

—*Josh Billings*

Necessity is the mother of deception.

—*Belle Sarnoff*

Decision-making

When a decision has been made and the die is cast, then murder the alternatives.

—*Mrs. Emory S. Adams, Jr.*

When the assistant football coach was made head coach, he was asked how he felt. He said, "I'm learning the difference between making recommendations and making decisions."

Decline

The horn of plenty, he said, is blowing taps.

—*Hon. Douglas M. Costle*

Dedication

I know the price of success—dedication, hard work and an unremitting devotion to the things you want to see happen.

—*Frank Lloyd Wright*

Defeat

Defeat can be the first step to something better.

—Edmund Burke

Difficulties

There are two ways of meeting difficulties: you alter the difficulties or you alter yourself to meet them.

Direction

If you do not change your direction you are likely to end up where you are headed.

—Ancient Chinese proverb

Discipline

No steam or gas ever drives anything until it is confined. No Niagara is ever turned into light and power until it is tunneled. No life ever grows until it is focused, dedicated, disciplined.

—Harry Emerson Fosdick

The price of excellence is discipline. The cost of mediocrity is disappointment.

—William A. Ward

Duty

It's not enough that we do our best; sometimes we have to do what's required.

—Winston Churchill

Editing

Remember not only to say the right thing in the right place, but far more difficult still, to leave unsaid the wrong thing at the tempting moment.

—Benjamin Franklin

Education

Education is a better safeguard of liberty than a standing army.

—Edward Everett Hale

History is rapidly becoming a race between education and catastrophe.

—H. G. Wells

Plato defined education as "the particular learning which leads you throughout your life to hate what should be hated and love what should be loved." What then should you love as much as you hate injustice and misery?

—Nicholas Gage

If you think education is expensive, think of the price of ignorance.

—John Gardner

Elegance

Elegance is good taste plus a dash of daring.

—Carmel Snow

Elephants

The Republican National Committee has selected New Orleans as the site of its 1988 convention. Not since Hannibal crossed the Alps has there been so much excitement about the arrival of elephants.

—Janice Aston

Enthusiasm

Every production of genius must be the production of enthusiasm.

—Disraeli

Error

I like John Gardner's story of the wife who read the fortune-telling card her husband got from a penny weighing machine. "You are a leader," she read, "with a magnetic personality and strong character—intelligent, witty and attractive to the opposite sex." Then she turned the card over and added, "It has your weight wrong too."

Evil

Think no evil, see no evil, hear no evil—and you will never write a best-selling novel.

—Dan Bennett

Example

Example is not the main thing in influencing others. It is the only thing.

—Albert Schweitzer

Experience

Just when you think you've graduated from the school of experience, someone thinks up a new course.

—Mary H. Waldrip

When a person with experience meets a person with money, the person with money will soon have experience.

—Leonard Lauder

Failure

Oscar Wilde arrived at his club one evening, after witnessing the first night of a play that was a complete flop.

"Oscar, how did your play go tonight?" asked a friend.

"Oh," came the lofty response, "the play was a great success, but the audience was a failure."

186

Faith
You can do very little with faith, but you can do nothing without it.

—*Samuel Butler*

Fame
Fame is proof that people are gullible.

—*Ralph Waldo Emerson*

Fashion
A fashion is nothing more than an induced epidemic.

—*George Bernard Shaw*

Designers have come up with clothes so ugly that hanging's too good for them.

—*L. A. Times Syndicate*

Fashion is a form of ugliness so intolerable that we have to alter it every six months.

—*Oscar Wilde*

Nothing in the world can replace the modern swimsuit, and it practically has.

—*Kirk Kirkpatrick*

Flexibility
A slender sapling will survive a storm by swaying with the wind. A rigid old branch will break off and die. We can learn a lot from trees.

—*Japanese proverb*

Friendship
Be civil to all, sociable to many, familiar with few.

—*Benjamin Franklin*

Friends are essential to success; they are still more essential to happiness. Therefore to win place and power and honor and happiness, begin by assiduously and unselfishly winning friends.

—B. C. Forbes

Love is blind—friendship tries not to notice.

—Otto Von Bismarck

You can make more friends in two months by becoming really interested in other people than you can in two years by trying to get other people interested in you.

—Dale Carnegie

Future

I try to be as philosophical as the old lady from Vermont who said that the best thing about the future is that it only comes one day at a time.

—Dean Acheson

The future belongs to those who see possibilities before they're perceived by others.

The trouble today is that the future isn't what it used to be.

Genius

Once when Paderewski played for Queen Victoria, she exclaimed with enthusiasm, "Mr. Paderewski, you are a genius!"

"Ah, Your Majesty," he replied, "perhaps, but before I was a genius, I was a drudge."

Genius means little more than the faculty of perceiving in an unhabitual way.

—William James

Goodwill

Goodwill cannot be purchased, it must be earned.

—Frank Tyger

Habits

Since habits become power, make them work for you and not against you.

—E. Stanley Jones

Hunting

A very good friend of mine is from this valley. He grew up the hard way and yet he built a substantial textile business. He worked so hard that he never enjoyed his youth, and upon reaching middle age he decided he would finally participate in the favorite local sport—hunting chamois.

The day he started to hunt, he walked all day deeper and deeper into the mountains and never saw a thing. Finally, toward dusk, he broke out into a clearing and there was a beautiful blond maiden sitting by a waterfall —without a stitch of clothing on! He stopped, astonished, and then asked her: "Are you game?" She replied, "Yes" —so he shot her!

—Harry A. Jacobs, Jr.

Ideals

Don't part company with your ideals. They are anchors in the storm.

—Arnold Glasow

It's not the crook in modern business that we fear, but the honest man who doesn't know what he's doing.

—Gwen Young

Ideas

Great ideas need landing gear as well as wings.

—Adolphe A. Berle, Jr.

Imagination

Often man deceives himself . . . very much like the gentleman who traveled everywhere with an odd-looking satchel and who one day when he sat down at a bar and ordered a drink was asked by the bartender, "Say, what's in that satchel?"

"A mongoose," the traveler replied.

"A mongoose? What for? Why carry around a mongoose?"

"Well, you see," said our gentleman, "I have a weakness. When I get to drinking I always see snakes. And when I see snakes, I open my satchel and let my mongoose out at them."

"But," said the bartender, "those snakes are only imaginary."

"So's my mongoose," the gentleman replied.

—Professor Nathan Resnick

Information

I find that a great part of the information I have was acquired by looking up something and finding something else on the way.

—Franklin P. Adams

Inventors

An inventor is an engineer who doesn't take his education too seriously.

—Charles Kettering

Involvement

In the city-state of Athens in ancient Greece, the philosopher Plato oberved: "It is the fate of all wise men who fail to participate in matters of government to be ruled by fools all the days of their lives." We must act promptly, firmly and cooperatively—otherwise, our industry and our nation may suffer precisely that fate.

—Paul McMullan

Job

Make your job important and it will return the favor.

—Arnold Glasow

Joy

Cheerfulness keeps up a kind of daylight in the mind and fills it with a steady and perpetual serenity.

—Joseph Addison

Judgment

Not all things have to be scrutinized, nor all friends tested, nor all enemies exposed and denounced.

—Spanish proverb

Kids

A man was shopping in a toy store with his two sons. Both boys were clamoring for electronic guns that made a loud, outerspacelike sound when fired, so the father picked up two. As the clerk rang up the sale, he said, "These things make a lot of noise. They'll drive you crazy." The man smiled a wicked little smile. "Not me," he replied. "The boys live with my ex-wife."

—James Dent
Charleston, West Virginia, Gazette

I was looking at a toy last week for my five-year-old granddaughter. "Isn't that rather complicated for a child of five?" I asked the salesman. "That, sir, is an educational toy, designed to prepare young people for life in today's world. Any way you put it together is wrong."

—*Frank H. T. Rhodes*

Knowledge

Knowledge is an antidote to fear.

—*Ralph Waldo Emerson*

Leader

The ambiance of the room changes when a leader walks into it.

Leadership

"The first and last task of a leader," John Gardner once wrote, "is to keep hope alive—the hope that we can finally find our way through to a better world—despite the day's bitter discouragement, despite the perplexities of social action, despite our own inertness and shallowness and wavering resolve." It is your commencement of that wonderful task that we celebrate today.

—*Frank H. T. Rhodes*

I suggest effective leadership calls for a minimum of blunders and a maximum of tact.

Leadership is the ability to get men to do what they don't want to and like it.

—*Harry S Truman*

The essence of leadership is to listen, learn, understand, evaluate, decide, communicate.

—*Francois Mitterand*

Learning

If you tell me I may listen,
If you show me I may understand,
If you involve me I will learn.

Liberty

Liberty means responsibility. That's why most men dread it.

—*George Bernard Shaw*

Life

Life is no brief candle to me; it is a sort of splendid torch which I have got hold of for the moment, and I want to make it burn as brightly as possible before handing it on to future generations.

—*George Bernard Shaw*

Listening

Why did God give man two ears and one mouth? So that he will hear more and talk less.

—*Leo Rosten*

A good listener is not only popular everywhere, but after a while he knows something.

—*Wilson Mizner*

Loneliness

Alone is not bad if together is not so good.

—*Lola Falana*

Loneliness, far from being a rare and curious phenomenon, peculiar to myself and to a few other solitary men, is the central and inevitable fact of human existence.

—*Thomas Wolfe*

What loneliness is more lonely than distrust?

—*George Eliot*

Love

If love is the answer, could you rephrase the question?

—*Lily Tomlin*

Love is a fruit in season at all times, and within reach of every hand.

—*Mother Teresa*

You must learn day by day, year by year, to broaden your horizon. The more things you love, the more you are interested in, the more you enjoy.

—*Ethel Barrymore*

Man

Man was made at the end of the week's work when God was tired.

—*Mark Twain*

Management

Management by objectives works better if you know the objectives. Ninety percent of the time you don't.

—*Peter Drucker*

The most important thing I ever learned about management is that the work must be done by other men.

—*Alfred P. Sloan*

Manners

Anyone can be heroic from time to time, but a gentleman is something you have to be all the time.

—*Luigi Pirandello*

Marriage

Keep your eyes wide open before marriage, and half-shut afterwards.

—*Benjamin Franklin*

Many a man in love with a dimple makes the mistake of marrying the whole girl.

—*Stephen Leacock*

The great secret of successful marriage is to treat all disasters as incidents and none of the incidents as disasters.

—*Harold Nicolson*

Maturity

Maturity is the ability to judge today's action in terms of its long-range cost.

—*John Gardner*

Memory

The composer Gounod had an incredible memory. When he was about nineteen he attended a rehearsal of *Romeo and Juliet* that was still in manuscript and being directed by the composer, Berlioz. The next day, when visiting Berlioz, he sat at the piano and played the entire finale from memory. The composer looked at him in astonishment. Had his work been pirated? Was it some incredible coincidence?

"Where the devil did you get that music?" he demanded.

"At your rehearsal yesterday," replied Gounod.

Mentality

On how many people's library shelves, as bottles of medicine, one might write: "For External Use Only."

Mistakes

He who would never make a mistake never made a discovery.

—*Samuel Smiles*

Only some of us learn by other people's mistakes. The rest of us have to be the other people.

—Chicago Tribune

Money

I've all the money I'll ever need if I die before 4 o'clock.

—*Henny Youngman*

There was a time when a fool and his money were soon parted, but now it happens to everybody.

—*Adlai Stevenson*

When I was young I used to think that money was the most important thing in life; now that I'm old, I know it is.

—*Oscar Wilde*

Make money your god and it will plague you like the devil.

—*Henry Fielding*

Morals

What is moral is what you feel good after and what is immoral is what you feel bad after.

—*Ernest Hemingway*

Mortality

Drive carefully! Remember it's not only a car that can be recalled by its maker.

—Consumers' Digest

Obesity

Message on a sweatshirt—*I'm fat and you're ugly, but I can diet.*

Objectivity

Rare is the person who can weigh the faults of others without putting his thumb on the scales.

—*Byron J. Langenfeld*

We do not see things as they are, we see things as we are.

—*the Talmud*

Obstacles

If you find a path with no obstacles, it probably doesn't lead anywhere.

—*Frank A. Clark*

Opinions

If in the last few years you haven't discarded a major opinion or acquired a new one, check your pulse. You may be dead.

He never chooses an opinion; he just wears whatever happens to be in style.

—*Leo Tolstoy*

Opportunity

The lure of the distant and difficult is deceptive. The great opportunity is where you are.

—*John Burroughs*

Opportunities are never lost. The other fellow takes those you missed.

Optimism

Optimism alone will be enough to carry us through the difficult times that lie ahead, and mindless optimism would be as foolish as the mindless pessimism of years past.

—*George P. Shultz*

Some people look at the world and say "why?"
Some people look at the world and say "why not?"

—*George Bernard Shaw*

What's the difference between an optimist and a pessimist? An optimist laughs to forget. A pessimist forgets to laugh.

Order

Order and simplification are the first steps to the mastery of a subject. The actual enemy is the unknown.

—*Thomas Mann*

Patience

If you are patient in one moment of anger, you will escape a hundred days of sorrow.

—*Chinese proverb*

Peace

We ought to engage in pursuits which are loving, not maligning; constructive, not destructive; orderly, not chaotic. Then we may feel that we have the right to a great peace and a great joy.

—*Malcolm Muggeridge*

Perception

You must look into people as well as at them.

—*Lord Chesterfield*

Perfectionism

Noel Coward wrote a postcard to his friend David Niven, who was an intense striver for perfection. On the card was a picture of the Venus de Milo. The message read, "This can happen to you if you keep on biting your nails."

—David Humes

Perseverance

'Tis known by the name of perseverance in a good cause, and of obstinacy in a bad one.

—Laurence Sterne

Persuasion

Let him who wants to move and convince others to be first moved and convinced himself.

—Thomas Carlyle

Pessimism

An optimist sees an opportunity in every calamity; a pessimist sees a calamity in every opportunity.

—Winston Churchill

Philosophy

Philosophy is nothing but sophisticated poetry to sum things up.

—Rabelais

Photograph

Fuchs' warning: If you actually look like your passport photo, you aren't well enough to travel.

—Sir Vivian Fuchs

Politics

A politician should have three hats—one for throwing in the ring, one for talking through, and one for pulling rabbits out of if elected.

—*Carl Sandburg*

A politician thinks of the next election, a statesman of the next generation.

—*James Freeman Clarke*

Harry Truman spent the first six months wondering how he made it to the Senate . . . and the rest of the term wondering how the others got there.

Have you ever seen a candidate talking to a rich person on television?

—*Art Buchwald*

Politics is the art of looking for trouble, finding it everywhere, diagnosing it incorrectly, and applying the wrong remedies.

—*Groucho Marx*

Politics is perhaps the only profession for which no preparation is thought necessary.

—*Robert Louis Steventon*

The mistake a lot of politicians make is in forgetting they've been appointed, and thinking they've been anointed.

—*Mrs. Claude Pepper*

Praise

Praise loudly, blame softly.

—*Catherine the Great*

Press

Nothing can now be believed which is seen in a newspaper. Truth itself becomes suspicious by being put in that polluted vehicle.

—*Thomas Jefferson*

Progress

Progress is not created by contented people.

—*Frank Tyger*

Reality

We can easily forgive a child who is afraid of the dark; the real tragedy of life is when men are afraid of the light.

—*Plato*

Religion

Going to church doesn't make a man a Christian any more than going into a garage makes a man an automobile.

—*Billy Sunday*

Remedy

Don't find fault, find a remedy.

—*Henry Ford*

Repentance

Bursting with news, a woman rushed to her neighbor's house. "Have you heard, Mrs. Smith? The minister's son has decided to become a jockey. Of course you know he was supposed to go to theological seminary this year."

Mrs. Smith, more a woman of the world than her friend, replied drily, "Well, I must say that he'll bring a lot more people to repentance that way than he would as a minister."

Reputation

Confessions may be good for the soul, but they are bad for the reputation.

—Thomas Robert Dewar

Research

When you take material from one writer it's called plagiarism; but when you take it from many writers it's called research.

—Wilson Mizner

Research is to medicine what sin is to confession. You can't have the latter without the former.

—Dr. Frank Rhodes

Respect

The respect of those you respect is worth more than the applause of the multitude.

—Arnold Glasow

Responsibility

Let everyone sweep in front of his door and the whole world will be clean.

—Goethe

You cannot help men permanently by doing for them what they could and should do for themselves.

—Abraham Lincoln

Rights

One trouble with the world is that so many people who stand up vigorously for their rights fall down miserably on their duties.

The right to do something doesn't mean that doing it is right.

Risk

The policy of being too cautious is the greatest risk of all.
—Jawaharlal Nehru

Who bravely dares must sometimes risk a fall.
—Tobias G. Smollett

Rumors

Rumors without a leg to stand on still have a way of getting around.
—Chicago Tribune

He who believes that where there's smoke there's fire hasn't tried cooking on a campfire.
—Changing Times

Secret

An older woman executive was being interviewed and when asked by the interviewer how old she was, she leaned toward him intimately and said, "Can you keep a secret?" He said, "Certainly." She leaned back and said, "So can I."

Sharing

Sharing is the great and imperative need of our time. An unshared life is not living.
—Steven Wise

Shyness

Shy people undervalue what they are and overvalue what they are not.

Smiles

Wrinkles should merely indicate where smiles have been.

—*Mark Twain*

Solutions

He who cannot describe the problem will never find the solution to that problem.

—*Confucius*

Sorrow

Sorrow is like a precious treasure, shown only to friends.

—*African proverb*

The swallows of sorrow may fly overhead, but don't let them nest in your hair.

—*Chinese proverb*

Speakers

I'm always a little suspicious of any group that pays a caterer fifteen dollars per person to fill their stomachs— and a speaker five cents a word to fill their minds.

Wise men talk because they have something to say, fools because they have to say something.

—*Plato*

Although the aim of a sculptor is to convince us that he is a sculptor, the aim of an orator is to convince us he is not an orator.

—*George Will*

It's never easy to be a substitute speaker. The audience looks on you the same way they look on making out their income tax. They hope for the best but they're prepared for the worst.

—*Robert Orben*

Speeches

A speech is like a wheel—the longer the spoke, the bigger the tire.

—Eunice Laughery

Spirit

Jeanne Moreau, when asked how long she expected to live, stated: "I shall die very young." She was asked, "How young?" "I don't know," she replied, "maybe seventy, eighty or ninety, but I shall die very young."

—Diana Vreeland

Standards

Good enough never is.

—Debra Field

Style

Style is self-expression with creativity and showmanship —something that makes you memorable and makes people want to imitate you.

—Eleanor Lambert

Substitution

Pinch-hitting giving a speech for David Ogilvy, our founder, makes me think that you must feel a little like someone who buys a ticket to see Laurence Olivier do *Hamlet* and after you arrive, when you're seated and open your program, a slip of paper announces that the role at that performance will be played by Henry Smythe instead of Olivier.

—Bill Phillips

Success

My cup runneth over—I'm only sorry that I don't have a saucer to catch the overflow.

—Dr. Stanley Sarnoff

Success often comes from not knowing your limitations.

—Frank Tyger

The man who lives for himself is a failure; the man who lives for others has achieved true success.

—Norman Vincent Peale

The only place success comes before work is in the dictionary.

To succeed is to leave the world a bit better by
A job well done—
Or a redeemed social condition—
To win the respect of intelligent people—
To earn the appreciation of critics—
To find the best in others—
And to know that even one life has breathed easier
Because you have lived.

—Ralph Waldo Emerson

Survival

If this nation is ever destroyed, it will not be from without but from within.

—Abraham Lincoln

Tact

Tact is the knack of making a point without making an enemy.

—Howard W. Newton

Talent

The weakest among us has a gift, however seemingly trivial, which is peculiar to him, and which worthily used, will be a gift to his race forever.

—John Ruskin

It took me fifteen years to discover I had no talent for writing, but I couldn't give it up because by that time I was too famous.

—Robert Benchley

A lad once asked Mozart how to write a symphony. Mozart said, "You're still very young. Why not start with ballads?"

The youngster replied, "But you composed symphonies when you were ten years old."

"Yes," said Mozart, "but I didn't have to ask how."

Talks

There is no merit in ninety-nine stories out of one hundred except the merit put into them by the teller's art.

—Mark Twain

Why doesn't the fellow who says "I'm no speechmaker" let it go at that instead of giving a demonstration?

—Frank Hubbard

Taxes

The income tax has made more liars out of Americans than golf has.

—Will Rogers

A sign in the window of a Cincinnati tax consultant: "Let us prepare your tax return and save you time—maybe twenty years."

—Wall Street Journal

Teaching

The art of being taught is the art of discovery, as the art of teaching is the art of assisting discovery to take place.

—*Mark Van Doren*

Television

Television is called a medium because it is rarely well done.

—*Goodman Ace*

Tenacity

Never give in . . . never, never, never, never . . . in nothing, great or small, large or petty—never give in, except to convictions of honor or good taste.

—*Winston Churchill*

Thinking

The real danger of our technological age is not so much that machines will begin to think like people, as that people will begin to think like machines.

—*Sidney J. Harris*

In order to acquire intellect one must need it. One loses it when it is no longer necessary.

—*Friedrich Nietzsche*

If you make people think they're thinking, they'll love you; but if you really make them think, they'll hate you.

—*Don Marquis*

Time

"I hear the boys are gonna strike," one worker told another. "What for?" asked the friend. "Shorter hours."

"Good for them. I always did think sixty minutes was too long for an hour."

—*Tal D. Bonham*

You will never find time for anything. If you want time, you must make it.

—*Charles Buston*

Trouble

Troubles, like babies, grow larger by nursing.

—*Lady Holland*

Never bear more than one kind of trouble at a time. Some people bear three—all they have had, all they have now, and all they expect to have.

—*Edward Everett Hale*

Truth

I tell the truth, not as much as I would but as much as I dare—and I dare more and more as I grow older.

—*Montaigne*

Values

It's reported that Sam Goldwyn telephoned George Bernard Shaw and tried to drive a bargain for the film rights to some of his plays. Shaw's terms were stiff and Goldwyn tried to whittle them down by an appeal to the artist.

"Think of the millions of people who'd get a chance to see your plays who would otherwise never see them. Think of the contribution it would be to art."

And Shaw replied: "The trouble is, Mr. Goldwyn, that you think of nothing but art and I think of nothing but money."

Victory

Part of the happiness of life consists not in fighting battles, but in avoiding them. A masterly retreat is in itself a victory.

—Norman Vincent Peale

Waiting

The longest wait in the world is when the nurse tells you to take off your clothes because the doctor will be with you in a moment.

—Ashley Cooper

War

Twenty-five centuries ago, the Chinese philosopher Sun Tzu wrote that fighting is the crudest and least satisfactory method of making war on an enemy. "Break the will of the enemy to fight," said Sun Tzu, "and you accomplish the true objective of war. The supreme excellence is not to win a hundred victories in a hundred battles. The supreme excellence is to defeat the armies of your enemy without ever having to fight them."

Weight

I'd better start watching my weight before others do.

Wisdom

A man begins cutting his wisdom teeth the first time he bites off more than he can chew.

—Herb Caen

A man should never be ashamed to own that he has been in the wrong, which is but saying in other words that he is wiser today than yesterday.

—Jonathan Swift

210

To my extreme mortification, I grow wiser every day.

—Lord Byron

Wit

Wit is the salt of conversation, not the food.

—William Hazlitt

Women

A woman is like a tea bag—you never know how strong she is until she gets into hot water.

Nancy Reagan

Back in the dark ages, women came to the office in silly little shoes and did all the work. Now they show up in track shoes and run the place.

—Rooster Sinclair

Women will be successful when no one will be surprised that they are successful.

—Leonard Lauder

Work

The ugliest of trades have their moments of pleasure. If I were a grave digger, or even a hangman, there are some people I could work for with a great deal of pleasure.

—Douglas Jerrold

When you are laboring for others, let it be with the same zeal as if it were for yourself.

—Confucius

Work spares us from three great evils: boredom, vice and need.

—Voltaire

Work itself is the reward. If I choose challenging work it will pay me back with interest. At least I'll be interested even if nobody else is. And this attempt for excellence is what sustains the most well lived and satisfying, successful lives.

—Meryl Streep

Worry

There is great beauty in going through life without anxiety or fear. Half our fears are baseless, and the other half discreditable.

—Christian Bovee

Worry is interest paid on trouble before it falls due.

—William Inge

212

Index